CAPITALIST IMPERIALISM,
CRISIS AND THE STATE

FUNDAMENTALS OF PURE AND APPLIED ECONOMICS

EDITORS IN CHIEF

J. LESOURNE, Conservatoire National des Arts et Métiers, Paris, France

H. SONNENSCHEIN, University of Pennsylvania, Philadelphia, PA, USA

ADVISORY BOARD

K. ARROW, Stanford, CA, USA

W. BAUMOL, Princeton, NJ, USA

W. A. LEWIS, Princeton, NJ, USA

S. TSURU, Tokyo, Japan

MARXIAN ECONOMICS I
In 3 Volumes

CAPITALIST IMPERIALISM, CRISIS AND THE STATE

JOHN WILLOUGHBY

ROUTLEDGE
Taylor & Francis Group

First published in 1986 by
Harwood Academic Publishers GmbH

Reprinted in 2001 by
Routledge
2 Park Square, Milton Park, Abingdon, Oxon, OX14 4RN
711 Third Avenue, New York, NY 10017

Routledge is an imprint of the Taylor & Francis Group, an informa business

Transferred to Digital Printing 2007

First issued in paperback 2013

The publishers have made every effort to contact authors/copyright holders
of the works reprinted in *Harwood Fundamentals of Pure & Applied Economics*.
This has not been possible in every case, however, and we would welcome
correspondence from those individuals/companies we have been unable to
trace.

These reprints are taken from original copies of each book. in many cases
the condition of these originals is not perfect. the publisher has gone to
great lengths to ensure the quality of these reprints, but wishes to point
out that certain characteristics of the original copies will, of necessity, be
apparent in reprints thereof.

British Library Cataloguing in Publication Data
A CIP catalogue record for this book
is available from the British Library

Capitalist Imperialism, Crisis and the State
ISBN 13: 978-0-415-26986-5 (hbk)
ISBN 13: 978-0-415-84634-9 (pbk)
Marxian Economics I: 3 Volumes
ISBN 13: 978-0-415-26983-0
Harwood Fundamentals of Pure & Applied Economics
ISBN 13: 978-0-415-26907-5

Capitalist Imperialism, Crisis and the State

John Willoughby
The American University, USA

A volume in the Marxian Economics section
edited by
John E. Roemer
University of California, Davis, USA

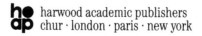 harwood academic publishers
chur · london · paris · new york

Harwood Academic Publishers

P.O. Box 197
London WC2E 9PX
England

58, rue Lhomond
75005 Paris
France

P.O. Box 786
Cooper Station
New York, NY 10276
United States of America

Library of Congress Cataloging-in-Publication Data
Willoughby, John, 1949–
    Capitalist imperialism, crisis, and the state.

    (Fundamentals of pure and applied economics; v. 7. Marxian economics section)
    Includes index.
    1. Imperialism.   2. Capitalism.   3. Marxian economics.   I. Title.   II. Series:
Fundamentals of pure and applied economics; v. 7.   III. Series: Fundamentals of
pure and applied economics. Marxian economics section.
JC359.W54   1986   325'.32   86-14967
ISBN 3-7186-0322-5

Contents

Introduction to the Series

Drawing on a personal network, an economist can still relatively easily stay well informed in the narrow field in which he works, but to keep up with the development of economics as a whole is a much more formidable challenge. Economists are confronted with difficulties associated with the rapid development of their discipline. There is a risk of "balkanisation" in economics, which may not be favorable to its development.

Fundamentals of Pure and Applied Economics has been created to meet this problem. The discipline of economics has been subdivided into sections (listed inside). These sections include short books, each surveying the state of the art in a given area.

Each book starts with the basic elements and goes as far as the most advanced results. Each should be useful to professors needing material for lectures, to graduate students looking for a global view of a particular subject, to professional economists wishing to keep up with the development of their science, and to researchers seeking convenient information on questions that incidentally appear in their work.

Each book is thus a presentation of the state of the art in a particular field rather than a step-by-step analysis of the development of the literature. Each is a high-level presentation but accessible to anyone with a solid background in economics, whether engaged in business, government, international organizations, teaching, or research in related fields.

Three aspects of *Fundamentals of Pure and Applied Economics* should be emphasized:

—First, the project covers the whole field of economics, not only theoretical or mathematical economics.

viii

—Second, the project is open-ended and the number of books is not predetermined. If new interesting areas appear, they will generate additional books.
—Last, all the books making up each section will later be grouped to constitute one or several volumes of an Encyclopedia of Economics.

The editors of the sections are outstanding economists who have selected as authors for the series some of the finest specialists in the world.

J. Lesourne   *H. Sonnenschein*

Capitalist Imperialism, Crisis and the State

JOHN WILLOUGHBY

Dept. of Economics, The American University, Washington D.C., USA

1. EVALUATING THE EARLY LENINIST THEORY OF IMPERIALISM

Introduction: The central role of Lenin in the development of the Marxist theory of Imperialism

What gives to Lenin's analysis of this new stage of development so much of its importance is that he clearly enunciated the respects in which this new stage modified or transformed certain of the relationships which were characteristic of the earlier pre-imperialist stage. [51, p. 246]

Apart from certain isolated cases, the efforts of Marxists, during the period when Lenin's conception of imperialism corresponded most closely to reality, were directed not so much towards refinement of his conceptual apparatus, as to mechanical and ritualistic repetition of his pronouncements. Lacking a sufficiently precise conceptual structure, they then found themselves unprepared to tackle even such macroscopic anomalies as those which became manifest after the Second World War. Instead of isolating and ordering these, to see... what their effective consequences for the paradigm were, Marxists took the course described above— *displacement of anomalies from the field of analysis into ever increasing ambiguities and imprecisions of language.* [15, p. 19]

The Marxian theory of imperialism inhabits a unique position in Marxian theory: the categories and hypotheses central to what is now the orthodox perspective do not originate with Marx or Engels, but rather were primarily formed during the first two decades of the twentieth century. One might say that this analysis of imperialism by Marxists represents the first systematic attempt to understand a

Acknowledgements: I would like to thank Wladimir Andreef, James Cypher and Shaun Hargreaves-Heap for their careful review of this manuscript. Micaeladi Leonardo and John Roemer provided me with important assistance at every stage of this project.

1

phenomenon never addressed in a sustained way in Marx's major work.[1]

At first, this lack of theoretical direction from the masters proved to be beneficial. Unlike the mechanistic theories of crisis characteristic of the Second International, the radical European theorists were explicitly engaged in an attempt to *apply* Marxism to a series of new events and structural shifts in advanced capitalism. In the case of Luxemburg, this led to a reconsideration of Marx's theory of expanded reproduction [121]. And Hilferding contributed much rich analytic detail to the Marxist conception of the concentration and centralization of capital [89]. Marxian economic theory in general was clarified and deepened as a result of these early "neo-Marxian" efforts.

Unfortunately, this creative adaptation of materialist theory came to a halt by the mid 1920s.[2] Two major events were responsible for this theoretical stagnation. Most fundamentally, the period of revolutionary socialist upheaval following World War I shattered the Marxist theoretical tradition of German Social Democracy. Karl Kautsky, the most prominent socialist theoretician of the pre-World I period, became isolated and was rendered almost irrelevant by the dual movements of Sparticist-inspired upsurge and Social Democratic management of capital's contradictions. And Rosa Luxemburg, the most creative thinker within German Marxism during this period, was assassinated while a leader of the newly-formed German Communist Party.

The second major event responsible for the death of creative Marxian thinking about imperialism was paradoxically the triumph of the Bolshevik Revolution. As the Soviet Union's party leaders began to exert their hegemony over the other national Communist Parties, Lenin's popular pamphlet on imperialism began to emerge

---

[1] V. G. Kiernan makes this clear in his excellent essay "The Marxist Theory of Imperialism and Its Historical Formation." See [104].

[2] One of the signs of Marxism's degeneration is the fate of those whose works which failed to follow the Soviet perspective slavishly. Fritz Sternberg's work *Der Imperialismus* [170] represents an extremely interesting attempt to integrate a labor-aristocracy theory with Luxemburg's original attempt to explain the necessity for capital expansion. Unfortunately, few Marxists even know about Sternberg's effort.

as a holy text.[3] Lenin's work on this subject is crucial in its own right. Many of his formulations remain central to our understanding of the concept today. On the other hand, this rigidification of theory has interrupted and deflected alternative radical attempts to understand more recent developments in the capitalist world economy. A new master, Lenin, emerged, and the peculiar necessity of Marxian thought to rely conservatively and exegetically on one source of wisdom for the development of its theory was reproduced.

A. Lenin's three arguments

If it were necessary to give the briefest possible definition of imperialism, we should have to say that imperialism is the monopoly stage of capitalism. [113, p. 85]

With this pithy statement, Lenin attempted to summarize sharply his view that imperialism is an inherent and inevitable outgrowth of the evolution of advanced capitalism. Monopoly emerges from the ongoing concentration and centralization process; this leads to the fusion of bank and industrial capital; and finally, the formation of these finance capital trusts stimulates, through intensified capital export, increased and intensified competition for monopolistic control over the territories of the world. This chain of reasoning is especially clear in Lenin's additional five-point description of imperialism:

1) The concentration of production and capital has developed to such a high stage that it has created monopolies which play a decisive role in economic life;

---

[3] Thus, Stalin writes:
Is it not true that the question of imperialism, the question of the spasmodic character of the development of imperialism, the question of the victory of socialism in one country, the question of the Soviet form of the state, the question of the role of the Party in the system of the dictatorship of the proletariat, the question of the paths of building socialism—that all these questions were elaborated precisely by Lenin? [169, p. 145]
Despite Lenin's contributions, it is precisely these issues that contemporary Marxism have *not* settled.

2) Bank capital has merged with industrial capital and created an oligarchy of finance capital;

3) The export of capital as distinguished from the export of commodities has acquired exceptional importance;

4) International monopoly capitalist associations have formed to share the world among themselves; and

5) The territorial division of the whole world among the biggest capitalist powers has been completed. [113, p. 86]

Points 1 and 2 refer to the structure of capitalist organization: the creation of monopolies and the rise of a financial oligarchy based simultaneously on industrial enterprises and banks. Point 3 argues that the form of international capital expansion is characterized by the export of money capital rather than increased commodity trade. And finally, points 4 and 5 stress the claim that this age of monopoly culminates in the division of the world among the major capitalist trusts and the nation-states that represent them.

Methodologically, this means that Lenin began at the economic "base" by focussing on the shifting organization of capital engendered by concentration and centralization. He then deduced the new forms of capital expansion which allow for much more extensive movements of capital into "external" territories. And *only then* did he discuss what we would more ordinarily consider to be imperialism: the attempts by dominant classes and "their" nation-states to establish control over external territories. For Lenin these moments of structural evolution, capital expansion and struggles for domination are so tightly and obviously linked to each other that he felt justified in labelling them all as *imperialism*. This is the first important innovation of the Leninist theory: *imperialism* is seen as a stage in the development of capitalism.

To reach a full understanding of Lenin's purpose in developing this theory of imperialism, however, it is necessary to delve further. The Bolshevik leader was not interested only in generally discussing the capitalist domination of the world economy. Rather, *Imperialism* was written to provide a political understanding of the specific results of this era of "monopoly capital" expansion. Beyond the general argument that advanced capitalism must lead to imperialism (and indeed is indistinguishable from imperialism) run two additional claims: that capitalist imperialism is characterized by chronic imperialist warfare, and that it culminates in the parasitic exploitation of backward economic regions by the advanced capitalist social formations. Lenin used these theoretical statements to strengthen his revolutionary socialist politics: only socialist revolution can free the globe from the related perils of misery and war.

In *Imperialism*, the second argument, that war is a central feature of monopoly capitalism, is more heavily stressed. This is hardly surprising, since Lenin wrote this pamphlet during World War I in order to argue against Kautsky's reformist perspective that there is no inevitable connection between capitalism and warfare.[4] To combat the Kautskyist position, Lenin maintained that capital accumulation is inherently uneven—in both a temporal and geographic sense. This implies that one can expect accumulation units in separately located territories to be differentially affected by capitalist growth, and thus booms and slumps can over time erode the competitive position of economic leaders and strengthen those firms positioned in more backward economic environments. From this postulate of an economic law of unevenness, Lenin then argued that no attempt to divide up the world among separate monopoly capitalist combines can ever be stable. Capitalist development will eventually make it advantageous for one firm to attempt to cut back the power of their erstwhile partners. This chronic economic tension will inevitably draft nation-states into the battle for economic territory. Thus, intensified competition among finance capitalist trusts leads to militarism and war among the major capitalist states—not just for resources in external, undeveloped regions, but eventually for territorial control over the capitalist world itself. In this sense, the logical structure of this capitalist rivalry argument is identical to the general claim that advanced capitalism is imperialism. An economic law is put forward (the law of uneven development), the effect of this law on firm behavior is deduced (the inability for any alliance of competitive enterprises to be stable), and the imperialist behavior of states is explained (imperialist rivalry and ultimately war).

---

[4] Kautsky argued for the formation of a trade union-liberal bourgeois alliance that would agitate for peace, while Lenin and Luxemburg campaigned for the mobilization of the proletariat for a revolutionary overthrow of the capitalist order. [193]

The third theme of imperialist parasitism is more difficult to derive from a particular economic law. Nevertheless, given Lenin's method, it is reasonable to attempt the discovery of an economic tendency which can serve as the "ultimate" cause of territorial exploitation. Fundamental to this search is the suggestion in *Imperialism* that the emergence of monopoly capitalism shifts the role that capitalism plays in world history: from being a progressive force of technological dynamism, monopoly negates the laws of competitive capitalism and ushers in a world of technological stagnation and intensified exploitation.[5] This theme appears in *Imperialism's* reference to both the rentier status of England's coupon clippers and the small "aristocracy of labor" that attains some of the benefits (through higher wages) of imperial exploitation. [113, p. 98]

In Lenin's hands, imperialism becomes a stage in capital's expansion, a system of implacable nation-state rivalry, and the routinization of territorial exploitation. None of these hypothesized features need contradict each other. On the other hand, it is important to assess this general neo-Marxist framework of analysis. It could be that particular flaws in theoretical reasoning and empirical analysis have weakened the connections among the complex of factors that Lenin outlined.

B. Early twentieth century theory: The confusion of Lenin's definition

Before proceeding to an assessment of Lenin's (and other early Marxists') detailed hypotheses, it is important to note that Lenin's own tendency to define advanced capitalism as imperialism constitutes a barrier to clear thinking. One could treat this "definition" as

---

[5] This is a more controversial interpretation of Lenin. He does argue that monopoly capitalism is a result of intensified competition. On the other hand, it seems clear that this competition is seen as parasitic rather than leading to progressive technical change. For Lenin, the transition from competitive to monopoly capitalist almost seems to lead to different laws of motion. Lenin writes the following:

As we have seen, the deepest economic foundation of imperialism is monopoly. This is capitalist monopoly; i.e., monopoly which has grown out of capitalism, commodity production and competition, in permanent and insoluble contradiction to this general environment. Nevertheless, like all monopoly, it inevitably engenders a tendency to stagnation and decay. [113, pp. 95–6]

what Arrighi calls a "hypothesized statement of fact"—which may or may not be true [15, pp. 10-1], but all too often advocates of the Leninst theory merely vaguely assert that imperialism is capitalism and therefore since capitalism exists so must imperialism. More sophisticated defenses rest on picking out that aspect of the Leninist theory that seems most valid, while ignoring the rest of the thesis.

Fortunately, there is a growing consensus among Marxian theorists that Lenin's definition must be abandoned if we are to understand the evolution of capitalist imperialism.[6] For this crucial purpose, Lenin's definition is both too general and too specific. It is too general because the definition leads us away from studying the specific phenomena of territorial domination/exploitation and nation-state conflict which most consider central to understanding imperialism today. It is too specific because far too many historically-situated aspects of early twentieth century international capitalism are seen as fundamental to a general theory of capitalist imperialism.

It is appropriate, therefore, to return to a more prosaic definition of imperialism that considers it as *attempted practices of domination over one territory and/or nation by the state and/or ruling elite which "represents" another territory or nation.* A theory of capitalist imperialism, then attempts to explain how the expansion of capital organizes global economic life and thereby contributes to imperial oppression and conflict. In this spirit, a more precise definition of capitalist imperialism (that should be treated carefully as a hypothesized statement of fact) is given by Peter Evans:

... a system of capital accumulation based on the export of capital from advanced countries to less developed regions (or more precisely center capital's acquisition of control over the means of production in those regions) accompanied by the utilization of political and military resources to protect and maintain the means of production over which control has been acquired [57, p. 16].

C. Early twentieth century theories continued: Reductionist flaws in the explanations of capital expansion

Lenin's attempt to explain imperialism through an examination of the laws of capitalist development is not unique. Most of the early radical writers assumed that if it were possible to identify a reason

---

[6] See Anthony Brewer for a clear criticism of Lenin's definition, [32, p. 110].

why capital *must* expand, then it would be self-evident that the state
would support this expansion in an imperialistic way; i.e. introduce
policies that would allow one state to control the political-economic
life of another. Because of this reductionist tradition, the Marxian
theory of imperialism is often considered solely as a radical theory
of capital expansion, which attempts to identify certain contradictions in the accumulation process impelling capital outward.
Modern commentaries on this subject, thus, often revolve around
an attempt to identify the "correct" contradiction—in the apparent
economistic belief that any examination of the political choice of
imperialist policies is unnecessary.[7]

There are two major problems with this approach. Most fundamentally, there is not a clear connection between any particular
contradiction which might cause capital to expand and the form
which imperialism might take. In a sense, the early theorists
demanded too much of themselves: the implicit method assumes
that one could deduce specific political behavior from a given set of
economic contradictions. This claim is highly problematic; a theory
of state behavior is crucial to any theory of imperialist conflict and
oppression.

The second problem, on which the contemporary literature has
tended to concentrate, is that few of the economic theories of
contradiction are persuasive in their own right. Rosa Luxemburg's
approach reveals in an extreme way the problems inherent in the
attempt to discover the "correct" barrier to accumulation. She
argued that capitalism contains within it a fatal flaw: the laws of
competition force each capital to attempt to expand and yet,
according to her, capital cannot survive without invading non-
capitalist areas of production. Because of an inevitable failure in
demand, the intensified outbreak of imperial tension is not due
fundamentally to any change in the organization of capital, but
rather to the desperate scramble for new "external" territories. (See
[121].)

It is now generally recognized that Luxemburg failed to prove
that there must always and necessarily be insufficient demand to
purchase the additional product that any expanding capitalist

---

[7] See in particular Tom Kemp's survey of early radical theories of imperialism
[101].

economy places on the market. Luxemburg had an unreasonably mechanistic model of realization because she misunderstood the elastic properties of credit extension and discounted the possibility of deficit financing by the state in the purchasing of military hardware. This does not mean that Luxemburg made no contribution to the theory of imperialism, but the point here is that her insights are swamped by her own methodology.[8] Luxemburg placed so much emphasis on the "inevitable" realization crisis that we are left with some profound description, but no serious explanation, of capitalist imperialism.

If we evaluated every early twentieth century radical theory of imperialism by the same criterion, (that there can be no effective explanation of imperialism without the correct identification of the cause of capital expansion), we would be forced to reach the same conclusion. *Luxemburg's failure is not unique.* Hobson, for instance, developed an under-consumptionist model of the realization crisis which maintains that the skewed distribution of income brought about by monopolization forces capital to attempt to export its excess product to external territories. This thesis rests on an empirical claim about the inability of the working class to agitate for higher real wages. Ironically, this premise was being contradicted by the formation of the first powerful general unions in Britain just at the time that Hobson was developing his thesis in [92].

The same criticism can be raised against the arguments that capital expansion is caused by chronic raw material shortage or working class militance.[9] There is no inherent reason why capital cannot overcome raw material difficulties through technological innovation, and indeed, the terms of trade between raw materials and industrial products do not exhibit any simple trend which suggests that advanced capitalism is plagued by this form of scarcity.[10] An argument about the determinants of working class

---

[8] One of Luxemburg's major contributions is that she specifically examines the role that debt plays in integrating non-capitalist sectors into the world economy.

[9] Karl Kautsky and Fritz Sternberg are especially associated with the raw material and class conflict theories of imperialism respectively. See [160] and [170].

[10] It could still be maintained that the general relative scarcity of raw materials is not as important as shortfalls in certain key commodities. While it is an important consideration for the capital penetration of any particular region, one cannot build a general theory of capital expansion on this basis.

opposition to the prerogatives of capital (either through wage conflicts or shop-floor struggles over the direction of production) is more complex. But it is clear that we cannot maintain that intense capital-labor conflict is necessarily associated with capital expansion.

Finally, the falling rate of profit thesis, which is important to Hilferding's analysis in *Finance Captial* [88, pp. 239–98], depends on Marx's original analysis of the tendency of the rate of profit to fall and the plausible observation that the new industries of the late nineteenth century and early twentieth century required massive amounts of fixed capital investment. We now know that if Marx's theory is viewed through comparative statics methodology then one cannot argue that capitalist evolution will produce a lower rate of profit unless the real wage also rises. (See [156].) Most early Marxian theorists did not realize this, and thus the explanation of capital export which rests on this "law" is seriously flawed.

Despite these shortcomings, the writings of the early theorists do allow the formulation of a more adequate accounting of capital expansion. In fact, Hilferding, Bukharin and Lenin actually articulated it, even while muddling their perspective with the search for the "fundamental" contradiction. If competition is viewed as constantly threatening the economic viability of any given accumulation unit, then it is clear that firms must always be engaged in a constant search for new ways to reorganize production, new markets and new input sources. This by no means, however, implies that the tendency for capitalism to expand is always expressed in the same way. Capital is constantly undergong social and technical reorganization. As finance capital emerges, the ability of monopoly capitalists to distribute their money capital to various accumulation projects expands. Moreover, this strengthening in the social power of the firm is necessarily coincident with massive developments in transportation, communication and military technologies, which make possible both expanded overseas investments and the launching of ambitious territorial conquests. In other words, the increasingly sophisticated evolution of capitalist technology (the forces of production) combines with new structural features of the giant capitalist enterprise to permit an intensifying foreign expansion of capital.

In the discussion of the simultaneous evolution of capital organization and the forces of production, the early twentieth century theorists emphasized the former, while Marx, writing before the maturation of finance capital, stressed the latter.

The bourgeoisie, by the rapid improvement of all instruments of production, by the immensely facilitated means of communication draws all, even the most barbarian, nations into civilization. [130, p. 477]

Nevertheless, it is possible to synthesize these differing emphases by noting that:

1) Capital inherently tends to expand because of the social relations of competition basic to its organization;

2) By the late nineteenth century, key developments in the forces of production (and destruction) permitted enterprises to exert more international control over their investment projects;

3) New organizational forms within and among accumulation units emerged to facilitate the exercise of this coercive power.[11]

These arguments were key to the early Marxist account of pre-World War I economic expansion. Nevertheless, it must also be said that the early theorists were reluctant to stay at this descriptive level. Realization crises, raw material shortages, chronic profitability pressures and even working class resistance to capitalist

---

[11] This approach permits a response to one further complaint. It has often been noted that Hilferding's and Lenin's description of finance capital suffers from its heavy emphasis on the development of Germanic investment banks. On superficial empirical grounds, the fusion of industrial and banking capital appears to have little to do with capital export because most foreign investments were organized by the City of London rather than the investment banks. (See [42].) This criticism, however, is not at all fatal to the Marxian understanding of finance capital. A good case can be made that the development of the City of London as the center of capital export is an indiciation of a new expansive power, which was manifested institutionally in Germany and the United States by the development of investment banks, and in Britain by the further maturation of the City of London. As North points out in [139, p. 159] some of the American investment banks were originally branches of English financial houses. A similar story could be told for France and Germany. (See [42, pp. 27 and 32].)

prerogatives are epiphenomena of the contradictions of accumulation, but nearly all radical theorists mistakenly rejected this perspective and attempted instead to identify one of these factors as a "fundamental" contradiction. This reductionist approach continues to breed confusion in Marxist theory today.

D. Did the early radicals understand the significance of capital export?

The findings of the previous section have serious consequences for any analysis of capital export to the Third World. It must be admitted that none of the theories of capital export offered compelling reasons for the *necessity* of the penetration of non-capitalist regions. Hobson's theory of under-consumption, Luxemburg's realization crisis analysis and Hilferding's falling rate of profit hypothesis suggest that capital will flow to "capital-poor" regions, but these precise formulations must be rejected. Even the theories of raw material scarcity or working class militancy do not automatically imply movements of capital outside of the advanced capitalist social formations. New raw materials might more readily be developed in capitalist territories where infrastructural investments are easier to mobilize, and the disruptions involved in the rapid creation of a modern proletariat make it unlikely that cheap labor can always be exploited in pre-capitalist social formations.[12]

This disposal of the arguments which predict the disproportionate flows of capital to "backward" economic regions are confirmed by the data. Money capital did not, by and large, flow to those territories in which capitalist social relations were not consolidated. Instead, much of it travelled to the rapidly expanding capitalist territories of Canada, the United States and Australia [42, p. 27]. The data indicate that the drive of competition which leads to capital expansion results in intensified accumulation within the capitalist territories themselves; it is not possible to maintain that capital will predominantly expand "outside itself."

Such a view is *not* foreign to some of the early theorists. Despite

---

[12] Gerschenkron makes this point especially clearly in [78].

his falling rate of profit thesis, Hilferding in particular emphasized the intensification of competition within the capitalist world, and Lenin stressed that imperialism involves more than competition over peripheral territories (see [89, pp. 301–10; and 113, p. 88].)

But this emphasis on sharpening inter-capitalist competition also missed an important point. Stressing the quantitative shares of capital flows downgrades the social impact of capital export to the periphery. The key role which economic expansion played in creating new capitalist nations in North America and Oceania has already been mentioned. Furtado has noted in [75] that the South American economies experienced a major social transformation as a result of the completion of infrastructural projects that allowed the intensified export of cash crops and mineral raw materials. India's economy did not experience as dramatic a transformation, but economic historians such as Gadgill [76] have stressed that the early twentieth century did witness the accelerated introduction of more advanced machinery and motors into factories. (As Marx had predicted, engineering and repair workshops began to emerge in response to the growing railway system.) It is also in this period that Europeans ceased to be content with maintaining trading posts on the coast of Africa and instead established colonial rule over the total continent. (See [63, pp. 251–383].) Finally and perhaps most significantly, capital export proved crucial to the capitalization projects of the governments and entrepreneurs of the European periphery—particularly Italy and Tsarist Russia. (See [79 and 80].)

In the late 19th and early twentieth centuries, capital did expand its influence everywhere. Despite the occasional theoretical and empirical hyperbole, it is justifiable to accept the neo-Marxist argument that imperialism is partly characterized by the increased flows of trade, finance and productive capital to capital-poor regions. Unfortunately, the recognition of this fact does not guarantee an adequate understanding of its significance. The traditional emphasis on capital flows tends to obscure the political and cultural dimensions of the creation of the capitalist world economy. The transformation of new networks of commodity production and distribution is associated with the simultaneous creation of new state structures and cultural identities. As we shall see, the early Marxist failure to grapple with this process lies at the root of its inadequate accounting of imperialist practices.

E. The crucial issue: Explaining pre-war capitalist imperialism

In order to provide a general framework of analysis, a theory of imperialism must be able to account for historical variety. Unlike other "imperialisms," the domination of other territories by capitalist powers has never been associated with one monolithic process, and this implies that the connection between capital export and imperialism is not at all straightforward. The failure to recognize this heterogeneous experience is the most glaring weakness in the early Marxist theory.

Of the territories external to Europe, for example, there are obvious counter-examples to the claim that capital expansion is always associated with intensified imperialism. To the extent that Britain's capital export assisted the capitalist development of North America, Oceania and South Africa, this weakened Britain's *imperial* influence even as it provided clear economic benefits to a significant sector of British capitalists.[13] For South America, most of Africa and Asia, the neo-Marxian argument is on stronger ground. The case of politically independent South America is complex, but there is a general consensus that Britain in particular established enough political hegemony over the region to determine the economic policies of the nominally independent states as well as to guarantee the security of the substantial British capitalist interests in the region.[14] Finally, there can be little argument that capital penetration in India, Indochina, China and Africa is associated with the intensified imperial control of these regions.

These historical examples strongly indicate that capital export *by itself* did not cause colonialism or other more subtle forms of imperialist domination in the pre-war era. Unfortunately, the Leninist theory in particular fails to grasp this conclusion. Instead, Lenin and Bukharin introduced a monolithic theory of rivalry and

---

[13] Certainly, important segments of British capital benefitted from capital export to the United States. But to the extent that capital export assisted the continental unification of North America, British capital export contributed to the building of a rival imperial pole.

[14] In 1914, British long-term investments in Latin America totaled $756.6 million. This compares with a $754.6 value for the United States and holdings worth $931.3 m in Canada, Australia and New Zealand. (See [63, p. 55].) There are some British historians who deny this assumption of British imperialism in Latin America. For a presentation and criticism of this perspective, see Tony Smith in [168, pp. 23–6].

parasitism that predicts the spread of capitalist colonialism to all sectors of the world economy.

This point can best be seen through a combined appraisal of the early theories of parasitism and rivalry. In *Imperialism,* Lenin maintained that the ability of modern capitalism to exert monopoly control over territories and industries heightens the tendency of capital to prey on rivals' fields of operations rather than attempting to compete through the development of the forces of production. This reliance on state power attains added importance because every capitalist enterprise's future is threatened by the erratic logic of accumulation. The temporally and spatially uneven nature of growth increases with advanced capitalism because capital's expansive power is so much greater. This forces even the largest accumulation units to demand the forceful political backing of "their" nation-state.

Finance capital and trusts have not diminished but increased the differences in the rate of growth of the various parts of the world economy. Once the relations of forces are changed, what other solution to the contradiction can be found *under capitalism* than that of force? (Lenin's emphasis in [113, p. 93].)

The basic problem with this thesis is revealed by the ease with which it can be reversed. Kautsky, for instance, suggested that the dominant characteristic of capital expansion is integration, not disruption, and this perspective led him to predict a unity of rather benign and progressive imperial interests. This rather implausible argument actually leads to a theoretical advance. Kautsky clearly realized that this hypothesis requires one to accept the possibility that the imperialism of the pre-World War I epoch and its associated militarism are *not* inevitable results of capitalist evolution.

The arms race rests on economic *causes* but not on economic *necessity.* Its suspension is in no way an *economic impossibility.* That in itself, however, tells us nothing about the *probability* of the advent of disarmament. Powerful classes have an interest in the arms race. Whether or not their resistance will be overcome is a question of political power. (Kautsky's emphasis in [160, p. 173].)[15]

---

[15] In a sense, Kautsky's approach is similar to Schumpeter's in his famous article "The Sociology of Imperialisms" [163]. For Schumpeter, imperialism only exists because of feudal, militaristic political elements which permit the flourishing of monopolistic interests. There are many anomalies in Schumpeter's theory—the most serious being the quite 'healthy' imperialistic impulse in the non-feudal United States. See [191] for documentation of this point.

This unity-rivalry conflict raises an important methodological point. It is impossible to analyze nation-state conflict without referring to the evolution of the capitalist state. Whether or not uneven development unifies or divides nation-states crucially depends on how they have been historically constructed within a specific international environment.

A closer look at the Marxian theories of the early twentieth century reveals that some of the authors did at times explicitly understand this argument. Hilferding, for instance, explained that the consolidation of the German nation-state in the late nineteenth century must be viewed in the framework of Britain's reigning imperial hegemony. It is in this context that protectionist tensions resulted in the imperialist fusion between finance capital and the rural Prussian aristocracy.

Lenin and Bukharin clearly wished to propose a less territorially-specific argument than Hilferding's. They maintained that there are forces at work which breed imperialism in *all* of the advanced capitalist social formations. Bukharin addressed this issue most directly. He hypothesized that uneven development will lead to militarized state capitalisms in all of the advanced capitalist social formations. Any disruption of the international basis of national accumulation leads to an internal and external mobilization of the nation-state's activities. This tightens the links between the military and capital even further, and moreover, the dependent middle strata are mobilized behind imperialist rhetoric to support even the most dangerous international adventures. The results of this process for the working class are also clear for Bukharin.

> With state capitalism making nearly every line of production important for the state, with nearly all branches of production serving the interests of war, prohibitive legislation is extended to the entire field of economic activities. The workers are deprived of the freedom to move, the right to strike, the right to belong to the so-called "subversive" parties, the right to choose an enterprise, etc. They are transformed into bondsmen attached, not to the land, but to the plant. They become white slaves of the predatory imperialist state, which has absorbed into its body all productive effort [34, pp. 159–60].

This formulation provides the deepest theoretical backing for Lenin's assertion that territorial domination and imperialist wars are inevitable features of advanced capitalism. For Bukharin, the instability of the global economy combined with the imperialistic merging of militarism and finance capital makes any rational calculation of the social costs and benefits of imperialism irrelevant; the prospects for a peaceful and progressive capitalism are minimal.

Despite the gripping power of Bukharin's prognosis, it is not necessarily superior to Kautsky's more prosaic perspective. Both visions are flawed by economic reductionism (with Kautsky emphasizing integration and the Leninists, uneven development). And consequently, both can only be more plausible if they are applied to specific historical environments in which the interaction between nation-state formation and world economic evolution can be observed more precisely.

This last criticism implies that the early Leninist attempts to explain the necessity of capitalist imperialism are incomplete. We cannot deduce capitalist rivalry from the logic of uneven development without additional arguments which connect the evolution of national social formations to the world accumulation process. And this, in turn, means that the roots of metropolitan territorial domination are still obscure. We have neither a general explanation of capitalist imperialism, nor an accounting of its heterogeneous character. This is a fundamental failure. No theory of imperialism can be complete without a compelling explanation of the varying forms of metropolitan capitalist state domination. And this requires an attention to the formation of varying political structures throughout the world economy—an attention which is diverted by the reductionist theories of capital expansion and, in the Leninist case, by the actual definition of imperialism itself.

Despite these harsh criticism, there are two key insights in Lenin's and others' works which are essential to the development of a more adequate Marxist explanation of capitalist imperialism.

1. Despite the tendency to overstress the quantitative intensity of capital flows between the "advanced" and "backward" sectors of the world economy, the early Marxist emphasis on the changing forms of capital expansion is crucially important. Finance capital and the related developments in the technologies of transportation, communication and warfare are fundamental to an analysis of the new dynamic power of capital in the pre-World War I period. For the first time, it was possible for firms to anticipate controlling

production and exchange in every corner of the globe. This is the kernal of truth in Lenin's claim that imperialism is characterized by the territorial division of the world economy among the major capitalist centers.

2. Most pre-war theorists recognized that it is necessary to explore the ways in which the international economy's evolution affects the economic and political reproduction of social relations in the advanced capitalist center. This insight is inadequate, for the social impact of capital penetration on the periphery was often ignored. Nevertheless, Hilferding's account of the industrialist/ Prussian alliance, Luxemburg's description of rising militarism, Lenin's cryptic analysis of the labor aristocracy, and Kautsky's hope for a liberal, professional middle class remain important features of contemporary analyses of imperialist politics.

Moreover, this attempt to link capitalist evolution to political and social structures provides a meeting ground for Marxist and non-Marxist theories of imperialism. Here, Veblen's, Weber's and even Schumpter's attempts to explain the culture of German imperialism can be connected to the early European Marxist stress on the logic of accumulation. A careful synthesis of these strands of thought can only enrich the materialist theory of imperialism.

2. TOWARDS A CONTEMPORARY MARXIAN THEORY OF IMPERIALISM

It is not easy to develop a theory of imperial oppression and conflict. The dynamics of capital expansion and capitalist state formation have both to be connected to the politics of imperialism.[16] Moreover, it is clear that all three processes in some sense mutually determine each other. How do we know where to begin?

Keat and Urry's recently articulated realist methodology of social science provides some guidelines for solving this problem. On the

---

[16] *Capitalist state formation* does not merely refer to the emergence of a political entity that is historically connected to the rise of capitalist social relations. This expression also means the continued development of the capitalist state as the economy and class relations evolve.

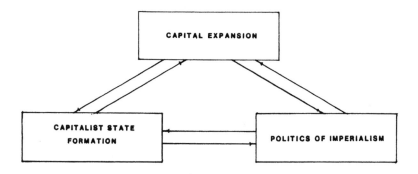

one hand, it is essential for Marxists to construct a theoretical system that is directly connected to the logic of capital accumulation. On the other hand, the problematic reasoning of the early Marxian literature stems from its economic reductionist methodology. The realist school suggests that the study of any social phenomena requires the construction of a theoretical model that, step-by-step, embraces more of the "real" world's dynamics.[17] It is necessary to begin with the abstract laws generated from within the contradictions of the mode of production before proceeding to a consideration of how these laws construct and deconstruct a more complex social formation or set of social formations. This method does *not* imply that the economic "base" must directly regulate all other arenas of social life. Rather, the claim is that the *understanding* of social processes can best begin with a study of the dominant social relations that organize material production and reproduction.[18]

---

[17] For Marx's description of this method, see [129, p. 100].

[18] A justification for this methodological claim can also be found in Russell Keat and John Urry, *Social Theory as Science* [100]. I would make the weaker argument that starting with an investigation of the capitalist mode of production is particularly important for studying the political economic evolution of the present world economy. It may well be that beginning at the economic "base" is inappropriate for studying the evolution of pre-capitalist social formations. In this case the organization of production is inextricably linked to the command over state-controlled "authoritative" resources. See [81].

In the case of imperialism, this approach suggests the following order of presentation.

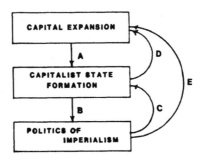

This schematic implies that the early theorists were correct in first studying the global expansion of capital—even if the search for the single contradiction that impels capital outward was misplaced. Analyzing the modalities of economic change in any given era provides the foundation for understanding capital internationalization's political impact.

How do capital expansion and nation-state evolution culminate in a systematic politics of territorial oppression and conflict? Answering this question is the ultimate goal of this investigation. The realist method, however, cautions against moving to this issue immediately, just as it warns against stopping too soon.

A. The internationalization of capital

Describing the internationalization of capital is less easy than would appear at first glance. For Marxists, *capital* is a term which embraces the key dynamic manifestations of the accumulation process—including trade, banking and productive investment and, most importantly, the creation of capitalist class structures.[19] One

---

[19] One common error in Marxist theory is the rhetorical conflation of terms. Thus, it is common to argue that capital *is* a social relation. This makes as much sense as claiming that snow *is* cold temperature. The generalized expansion of capital is predicated on the existence of certain social relations, but capital is not proletariat-bourgeois conflict itself. Rather, this term stands for those resources (human, physical, financial) that are employed in the attempted creation (or capturing) of surplus value.

cannot trace capital export by focussing on one variable. Moreover, following the paths of internationalization requires a regional perspective even though capital itself is a category which most abstractly eschews any geographically-bounded identification. Any empirical approach to this issue is bound to be makeshift. Data limitations, for instance, require the utilization of national categories to examine the logic of uneven development even though nationality should not be introduced at this stage of the analysis. Even more severe empirical constraints require the viewing of the proletarianization process in the Third World from information on the distribution of national populations between urban and rural sectors.

The most straight-forward beginning is to disaggregate the forms of capital expansion. Marx himself suggests that expanded reproduction (the "quantitative" aspect of the valorization process) can be conceived as a series of three interlocking moments: the money capital circuit $\left(M - \frac{LP}{MP} - P \longrightarrow C' - M'\right)$; the productive capital circuit $\left(P \longrightarrow C - M \longrightarrow \frac{LP}{MP} \longrightarrow P'\right)$; and the commodity capital circuit $\left(C - M - \frac{LP}{MP} \longrightarrow P \longrightarrow C'\right)$.[20] Since Rudolf Hilferding's *Finance Capital* [88], this framework has been employed in analyses of the world economy and Christian Palloix, in particular, is known for his contemporary adaptation of this schema. In Palloix's early studies, there is an evolutionary story implicit in his presentations. (See [144].) The growth of the capitalist world economy begins with the internationalization of commodity capital (the growth of international trade), proceeds to the internationalization of money capital (portfolio and banking investments) and concludes with the internationalization of productive capital (direct foreign investment). This stylized history is only plausible if one ignores the inter-war period of the twentieth century (in which trade and lending collapsed) and the 1970s (in

---

[20] Marx developed this terminology and representation in [127, pp. 109–79]. *M* represents money capital; *P*—productive capital; and *C*—commodity capital. *LP* and *MP* stand for *labor power* and *means of production* respectively.

which the growth in the volume of lending clearly outstripped expansions of the more 'advanced' productive capital circuit). Because of these anomalies, it is not my purpose to make a linear historical argument while using these distinctions. Rather, Marx's reproduction circuits are useful in empirically disentangling the complex networks of accumulation that presently exist in the world economy.

The internationalization of commodity capital: multilateralization and uneven development within the core
Most discussions of commercial trends in the global economy since the close of World War II begin with two important observations: the relative share of trade in global production has risen substantially for the advanced capitalist nations, while the proportion of commerce flowing to and from the United States has declined. Tables I and II provide documentation of both these points.

It appears that this most recent period of unprecedented capitalist expansion is similar to the one that preceded the outbreak of World War I. Then, world trade also grew at a faster pace than national production, and the United States and German capital were effectively challenging Britain's international commercial hegemony. It would be a mistake, however, to overstate the similarities between these two periods. Multilateral trade networks between the European imperial center and the Southern territories were strictly limited by the spreading reality of colonial control over Africa and Asia. There was always the imminent possibility (which Lenin in particular stressed) of breakdown and the subsequent creation of rival imperial zones. The inter-war period bears somber witness to this potential. This collapse has not been characteristic of the 1970s. Despite deep recessions, high inflation and sluggish growth, trade has both continued to expand more rapidly than domestic production and becomes even more multilaterialized.[21] Uneven development is a powerful reality of the capitalist world economy, but speculating about the possible manifestations of this contradiction during periods of crisis requires a more thorough, historically-sensitive analysis.

---

[21] For a report on trends through the late 1970s, see [192, pp. 195–211].

TABLE I
Exports and imports as percentages of GDP

	Exports			Imports		
	1960–6	1967–73	1974–80	1960–6	1967–73	1974–80
USA	5.1	5.6	8.7	4.4	5.6	9.4
Japan	9.9	10.5	12.9	9.7	9.2	12.6
FRG	18.2	21.1	25.9	16.6	18.4	23.8
France	13.8	15.8	21.2	12.9	15.1	21.6
UK	20.2	22.5	28.8	20.9	22.6	29.2
Italy	14.8	17.8	25.1	14.4	17.0	25.6
Canada	18.9	22.5	28.8	18.9	21.1	25.4
Total	9.7	11.1	15.8	9.1	10.6	15.8

Source: OECD Economic Outlook: Historical Statistics 1960–80 (Paris: OECD, 1982): 63.

The internationalization of productive capital: The intensification of integration and uneven development
Data ambiguities require a skeptical handling of quantitative reports of investment trends. (Trade figures certainly cannot be accepted with complete confidence, but foreign commerce accounting is less subject to error and more regularly available in the reports of

TABLE II
Shares of trade

	Exports as Percentage of OECD Exports		
	1962–6	1967–73	1974–80
USA	20.4	18.2	17.8
Canada	6.1	6.3	5.5
North America	26.5	24.5	23.3
Japan	4.8	7.1	9.8
EEC	51.8	51.7	52.2
	Imports as Percentage of OECD Imports		
	1962–6	1967–73	1974–80
USA	20.7	20.9	18.7
Canada	5.0	5.1	5.4
North America	25.7	26.0	24.1
Japan	5.9	8.1	8.9
EEC	51.1	50.1	51.4

Source: OECD, *National Accounts, 1951–80, vol. I* (Paris: OECD, 1982): 87. Computed from data in 1975 prices and 1975 exchange rates.

TABLE III

	Percentage distribution of US capital exports (flows)						
	1953	1956	1966	1973	1979	1982	1983
Direct foreign investment	101.1	61.7	84.1	34.4	42.8	−2.8‡	17.6§
Portfolio investment	−23.4	9.7	11.4	5.7	8.2	7.4	17.3
Other financial investment†	21.9	28.6	4.5	59.9	49.1	95.4	57.8

Source: Various issues of Survey of Current Business (March 1955, March 1958, March 1975, March 1981, March 1984).

† Other financial investments include short-term and long-term claims by U.S. banks and other private institutions.

‡ 1982 was a peculiar year because of a $8.3 b. inflow in equity and inter-company accounts from the Netherland Antilles. If this is excluded from Direct foreign investment figures, the DFI outflow would have been $6.5 b.

§ The corresponding disinvestment from the Netherland Antilles was "only" $1.8 b. in 1983. The DFI outflow figure would have been $12.4 b. if this inflow had been excluded from the accounts.

international agencies such as the OECD, IMF and UN.) Despite these problems, it is possible to summarize key aspects of productive capital export. Table III, for instance, indicates that direct foreign investment represented the largest type of capital export (not including trade) from the US until the mid-1960s. (In contrast, British capital exports before World War I primarily took the form of money capital portfolio investments.)

As direct foreign investment grew in absolute terms, the focus of US transnational corporate activity shifted away from its traditional locations in Latin America and Canada and towards Europe. This result parallels the increasing concentration of trade within the advanced capitalist world during the 1950s and 1960s. In the 1970s, the trend reversed itself and the Third World became a slightly greater focus of productive capital investment. This result is not surprising. Most theories would predict that foreign investment and trade movements should complement each other.[22]

[22] Even Raymond Vernon's early 1970s product cycle hypothesis, which suggests that Direct Foreign Investment *replaces* exports, can be modified to take account of the significant presence of intra-company trade in the modern world economy. See [185, pp. 65–77]. For data on the distribution of foreign investment between advanced capitalist and Third World territories, see [141, p. 54].

TABLE IV

	Geographical position of US direct foreign investment abroad†				
	1953	1956	1966	1973	1979
Canada	32.9	34.6	30.3	25.2	21.3
Europe	14.6	15.8	31.6	37.8	42.3
Other developed	4.1	4.5	6.2	8.3	8.0
Latin America	35.5	32.4	18.8	16.3	19.1
Other developing	9.8	9.0	7.9	6.3	5.7
Developed	51.7	55.0	68.1	71.3	71.6
Developing	45.5	41.4	26.8	22.6	24.8

Source: Obie G. Wichard, "Trends in U.S. Direct Investment Abroad," *Survey of Current Business* **61** (February 1981): 50–1.

† Figures do not add up to 100 because unallocated and international categories are not included.

The process of uneven development is also indicated by foreign investment data. The US is no longer the *only* major home of transnational enterprise. Indeed, the domestic American economy itself has become a major "host" zone for capital export. Rival national corporations clearly possess the technological and marketing abilities to compete with previously dominant US businesses on their own terms. As a result, each national economy has become more interlocked with most others. In the modern period, uneven development is strikingly associated with metropolitan capital inter-penetration—both within the core and periphery.

The internationalization of money capital: the differentiation of the periphery
The post-1945 epoch is not just distinct because of the major importance of direct foreign investment and the related shifts in trading activity. Contemporary capitalism has been maintained and extended by the globalization of the money capital circuit as well. Because of the enormous rise of lending during the 1970s, some analysts have been tempted to suggest that the importance of direct foreign investment is receding. The OECD, for instance, has

TABLE V

| | Outward direct investment flows | | |
| | Percentage distribution among predominant industrial capitalist countries† | | |
	1961–7	1968–73	1974–8
Canada	2.3	4.5	6.2
US	61.1	45.8	29.3
Original EEC‡	22.4	29.2	42.6
UK	8.7	9.1	9.2
Japan	2.4	6.7	13.0
Other Europe &Asia§	2.7	4.4	6.8

See Table VI for notes.

TABLE VI

| | Inward direct investment flows | | |
| | Percentage distribution among predominant industrial capitalist countries† | | |
	1961–7	1968–73	1974–8
Canada	16.1	12.1	3.2
US	2.6	11.4	26.7
Original EEC‡	50.2	47.5	50.4
UK	9.7	7.4	6.1
Japan	2.0	1.7	1.2
Other Europe & Asia§	21.5	19.7	17.8

Source: OECD, *International Investment and Multinational Enterprise: Recent International Direct Investment Trends* (Paris: OECD, 1981).

† The U.K. & U.S. data do not include re-invested profits in order to keep national data comparable. The UK data do *not* include the petroleum sector.

‡ Belgium, France, Germany, Italy, Luxemburg, the Netherlands

§ Australia, Norway, Spain, Sweden

concluded that:

> Multinational firms may be tending increasingly to focus on the provision of technology, marketing arrangements and certain aspects of management as their source of profit, relegating control of the purely financial dimension of international investment to financial organizations and the managerial aspects as well as legal ownership to their host country associates.[23]

This argument is premature. The aggregate rate of direct foreign investment growth has not slackened until recently, and new arenas of accumulation have emerged at the same time that metropolitan capital has withdrawn from others.[24] It is true that metropolitan bank lending has become an increasingly important form of capital export, but this should not be considered competitive with productive capital export. For these reasons, Andreef makes a compelling argument in [13] that international capital's total position in the world economy has never been stronger.

The internationalization of money capital does add a qualitatively new dimension to global capitalism, but not because direct foreign investment has lost its force. Rather, the extension of bank lending is directly associated with the sharp differentiation of the periphery. It is during the 1970s that Third World oil-exporting nations acquired a particular, short-term economic power; that commentators began to note the emergence of "newly industrializing countries" (NICs) in Latin America and East Asia; that categories such as *least developed* and *basic needs* countries acquired currency. If the evolution of the world economy is viewed by tracking changing financial flow patterns, these rhetorical divisions of the Third World become less arbitrary. The rapid expansion of bank capital was almost solely directed to the NICs, and after each of the two oil price shocks of 1974 and 1979, OPEC nations for a short time afterwards actually provided money capital to the world economy. For the rest of the Third World, "official development

---

[23] Cited in [141, pp. 28–9].

[24] This repositioning of metropolitan capital is not just geographic, but also sectoral. Peter Evans has especially stressed the role that evolving market structure plays in regulating the "triple alliance" among Third World states, local capitalists and multinational capital. See [57].

assistance" sponsored by a single industrial nation-state, by a grouping of states (such as the EEC) or by multilateral institutions, has continued to play the major role in integrating these less dynamic territories with the world economy.

TABLE VII

| | Percentage shares of total resource flows to different categories of developing countries, 1981 | | | | |
	NICs	MICs	OPEC	LICs	Total
Total Resource Flows ($86.8)	37.9	31.9	0.9	29.3	100.0
Official Development Assistance ($28.1)	2.8	36.3	1.1	59.8	100.0
Non-concessional ($58.7)	54.7	29.8	0.8	14.7	100.0
Bank Lending	88.9	22.7	−9.9	−1.7	100.0
Export Credits	34.9	29.8	8.5	26.8	100.0
Direct Investment	44.4	27.4	2.1	26.0	100.0
Multilateral	34.5	47.0	0.9	17.6	100.0

Allocated amounts based on preliminary estimates. Totals exclude some bond issues.

Low income countries (LICs) had GNP *per capita* below $600 in 1980.

Middle income countries (MICs) had GNP *per capita* above $600.

Newly industrialized countries (NICs) are Argentina, Brazil, Greece, Hong Kong, S. Korea, Mexico, Portugal, Singapore, Spain, Taiwan, and Yugoslavia.

The OPEC category does not include Indonesia (a LIC) and Nigeria (a MIC).

Source: *World Economic Interdependence and the Evolving North-South Relationship* (Paris: OCED, 1983):67.

The concentration and centralization of capital: finance capital's maturation and the proletarianization of the periphery

The capital circuit approach to studying the internationalization of capital is largely useful in describing the contradictory processes of integration/differentiation that are basic to the accumulation dynamic. This focus on the quantitative logic of expanded reproduction, however, cannot directly illuminate those qualitative shifts in the material organization of economic life that have resulted from post-war economic expansion. For this project, it is necessary to turn to another aspect of Marx's analysis and focus instead on what Marx called the concentration and centralization of capital.

Normally, this term refers to the increase in the average size of accumulation units (concentration) and their merger into large monopoly or finance capitalist enterprises (centralization). Hilferding, for instance, argued that this process changes the nature of inter-capitalist competition because the successful valorization of capital becomes pre-eminently associated with money capital/conglomerate management.[25] In the post-war period, technological breakthroughs have made this early twentieth century thesis even more compelling: it is now possible to control global production and marketing operations from a single managerial center. One key result of the post-war expansion has, thus, been the rise of the transnational corporation; its power is a fundamental aspect of modern capitalism.[26] In other words, a key aspect of the multilaterialization of international capitalist competition in the post-war period has been the concomitant centralization of corporate power. The networks of capitalism are simultaneously more diffused and more tightly linked; the continuous extension of global competition increasingly requires the hierarchical organization of the firm.

This transformation of both the internal structures of capitalist firms and their relations to each other is one aspect of the concentration and centralization dynamic. Marx maintained in most of his mature writings, however, that the most profound impact of progressive accumulation is the stripping of pre-capitalist producers from direct access to the means of production. If he is correct, then the obverse side of the rise of the transnational corporation is the proletarianization of the mass of laborers, for as Marx argued in [126, pp. 776–7]:

With the increasing mass of wealth which functions as capital, accumulation increases the concentration of that in the hands of individual capitalists, and thereby widens the basis of production on a large scale and *extends the specifically capitalist*

---

[25] ... It (the industrial corporation) converts what had been an occasional, accidental occurrence in the individual enterprise into a fundamental principle: namely, the liberation of the industrial capitalist from his function as industrial entrepreneur (See [89, p. 107].)

[26] The late Stephen Hymer deserves credit for being one of the first to make this compelling argument. (See [94, pp. 113–140].)

methods of production . . . Accumulation therefore presents itself on the one hand as increasing concentration of the means of production, *and of the command over labor*; and on the other, and as repulsion of many capitals from one another. (my emphasis)

Since Marx's time, new theories have developed which suggest several intermediate stages between the uprooting of pre-capitalist-contact social relations and the formation of a wage-labor class. Rosa Luxemburg, for example, recognized in [121, pp. 368–418] that capital penetration creates several different "economies" before finally dissolving all pre-capitalist social relations. And, more recently, a complex literature has emerged which attempts to trace out the articulation of different modes of production within a social formation. There is an important debate within this literature about the stability of these linkages—whether capitalism tends to dissolve these social relations, or whether, instead, precapitalist modes of production intensify in order to maintain political order and even enhance exploitation.[27] The intensification of certain exploitative pre-capitalist social relations may have been one result of previous periods of capital penetration. Today, however, subsistence agriculture is rapidly declining; the relative share of the urban population has increased in all sectors of the world; and a new caste of low-wage workers from the periphery of Europe and North America has migrated to the more dynamic sectors of the metropolitan capitalist economies. There can be little doubt that we are currently living in an epoch of global proletarianization.[28]

Hand in hand with this generation of a new working class (with its attendant reserve army) has been the appearance of a much larger professional elite in the Third World. Once again, good, direct evidence of this phenomenon is not available. Nevertheless, both the enormous rise in higher education and the staffing of the expanding Third World state with indigenous peoples are clear indications of this class's important position in the Third World.[29] Indeed, most recent theories of the peripheral, post-colonial state

[27] For the most detailed English-language discussion of this issue, see [175].

[28] For information on immigration to the advanced capitalist world, see [109 and 52].

[29] Between 1970 and 1980, enrollments in higher education in the Third World increased in most countries by well over 100 percent. See [182, pp. 248–78].

TABLE VIII

	Urbanization rates and urban population growth, 1950–2000					
	Urban population as percentage of total population			Average annual percentage growth or urban population		
	1950	1975	2000	1950–60	1970–80	1990–2000
Developing countries	20.6	31.1	45.8	4.0	4.0	3.5
Industrial capitalist countries	62.4	74.4	83.6	2.0	1.2	0.8
World	29.0	39.3	51.5	3.5	2.8	2.6

Source: OECD, *World Economic Interdependence and the Evolving North-South Relationship* (Paris: OECD, 1983): 81.

focus on the politically ambiguous class relation of this group to metropolitan imperialism.

Conclusion
This quantitative and qualitative analysis of post-war capital expansion provides the basis for a more thorough understanding of contemporary imperialism. More specifically, there are five key findings to keep in mind.

1) The internationalization of capital is presently associated with the multilateralization of economic life. Spheres of national capitalist influence are in decline, both within most metropolitan economies and in the capitalist Third World.

2) As in previous eras, capital evolution is linked to uneven development. In particular, the leading role of the United States economy in the world accumulation process has quantitatively declined, while the relative levels of capitalist production in Europe and Japan have correspondingly risen.

3) This dynamic of uneven development has strikingly extended itself to the Third World. Money and productive capital have predominantly flowed between the "Newly Industrializing Countries" (NICs) and the metropolitan economies, while the more "backward" territories are still primarily integrated into the capitalist world economy through "foreign assistance."

4) The international capitalist firm has taken on more of the attributes first delineated by Rudolf Hilferding in *Finance Capital*. The global extension of the operations of private enterprise is associated with the consolidation of the transnational corporation. And these industrial and financial combines are now directly involved in managing all aspects of the circuit of expanded reproduction.

5) The intensified expansion of capital into the periphery has created a proletarianized laboring population and an enlarged professional class. These social transformations have profound significance for any explanation of contemporary capitalist imperialism.

B. Capital expansion and post-war theories of capitalist state formation

Introduction
The preceding analysis of post-war capital export is not controversial. Many contemporary theorists have noted the same trends, and even Marx's initial discussion of capitalism's international impact can be read as an analysis of the rise of monopoly capital and the spread of the proletariat. At this most abstract level of understanding the expansion of capital, much of the tradition of Marxian economics need not be altered radically. Rather, Marxism remains a powerful analytic method.

This consensus breaks down, however, when the impact of capital export on politics within metropolitan and peripheral national social formations is considered. Here, theoretical and ideological debates are quite intense; it is difficult to investigate the connections between capital internationalization and nation-state formation dispassionately.

The first step in a systematic study of this problem is to assess the relative power of capital internationalization in determining the political structures and actions of capitalist social formations. Although the premise of such an exercise is that a regional economy's position within the global accumulation process will significantly determine local and inter-regional political interventions, I am not claiming that *all* key characteristics of the political

within the world economy should or can be deduced from the logic
of accumulation. Rather, the argument is that opening the analysis
with a study of the political impact of capital expansion is crucial to
the development of a materialist understanding of capitalist imperialist politics. On a more general level, it is not possible to
explain the interrelations between the "political" and the "economic" without first conceptually separating these two arenas of social
practice. For this reason, determining the level of abstraction
appropriate for studying metropolitan and peripheral state formations is one of this section's key tasks.

Capital expansion and metropolitan state formation
During the post-war period, Marxist explanations of the imperialist
state have been most fully developed by the state monopoly
capitalist, radical dependency and world systems schools. There are
two tendencies in accumulation emphasized by the state monopoly
capitalist paradigm. On the one hand, it is posited that the
centralization of capital has permitted the articulation of Keynesian
welfare and directly corporatist mechanisms of national political
regulation. As a result, the links between national monopolies and
the state have become even more tightly forged than during the
pre-World War I era of monopoly capitalism. When considered
alone, this hypothesized process has few implications for a theory of
imperial state formation. Indeed, some have used this tendency to
argue for the possibility of a progressive Social Democratic or
Eurocommunist exit out of imperialist capitalism.[30]

The second strand of the state monopoly analysis, however, takes
issue with this Kautskyist conclusion; it is argued that uneven
development or the anarchy of global competition prevents such a
reformist consolidation. Instead, shifts in political-economic power
force individual advanced capitalist states, or alliances of capitalist
states, to take measures to protect the integrity of "its" or "their"
units of finance capital. The result of these struggles determines the
overall mechanism of global capitalist regulation, and it is possible
on this basis to periodize capitalist imperialism. For this project, the
key task is to note accurately the crucial historically-significant shifts
in advanced capitalist nation-state relations.[31] More will be said

---

[30] Carl Boggs provides an interesting review of this perspective in [27].
[31] For a sample of this regulatory approach, see Alain Lipietz in [118].

about this method in the discussion of imperial crisis. For now, it is most important to note that these state monopoly capitalist approaches represent a partial elaboration of the original Leninist theory. Imperialist practices are derived from the interaction of the national centralization of capital with global uneven development.

The world systems and radical dependency schools address this issue from a different perspective. Rather than focussing on the centralization of national capitals under the aegis of rival metropolitan nation-states, Samir Amin, Andre Gunder Frank and Immanuel Wallerstein all place their emphasis on the extraction of surplus from the periphery. In this perspective, imperial structures and practices are linked to the dynamics of center-periphery exploitation; the Keynesian welfare state is an epiphenomenon of the creation of a privileged mass of workers in the core. Amin, in particular, argues that parliamentary democracy in the West masks the brutalization and impoverishment of the mass of productive workers in the periphery.[32]

One distinct result of this approach is a slackening stress on nation-state structures and an increased concern with transnational metropolitan institutions—from the private multinational corporation to international organizations. It is implicitly posited that the centralization of capital does not lead to the strengthening of individual nation-state units; instead the interpenetration of capitals stimulates the construction of new unifying regulatory mechanisms. For this approach, the fundamental contradiction within global capitalism lies between North and South, rather than within rival centers of the advanced capitalist world.

It is possible to synthesize the state monopoly capitalist and world systems dependency perspective. In speculating about global imperialism's future, Frank and Wallerstein both maintain in [69 and 186] that uneven development combined with Third World resistance makes political economic rivalry among metropolitan capitalist political entities more likely. In this scenario, the decline

---

[32] But with the advent of imperialism, whether in the form of imperial preserves or of a world ostensibly open to all, the international division of labor between centers and peripheries takes on a new dimension. My basic thesis is that this new division of labor ushers in the era of the social-democratic alliance in the imperialist center. (See [6, p. 26].)

of the United States will unleash a new round of competitive alliance building, and the Third World will play a key role in determining the nature of a reorganized global system.

Unfortunately, this synthesis represents the worst of both worlds. It combines the dubious premise that the centralization of finance capital is coterminous with the territorial authority of the nation-state with the questionable assumption that the politics of Third World nationalism is necessarily resistant to the prerogatives of metropolitan capital.

The first premise clearly flies in the face of the data presented in the previous section. The international interpenetration of capitals suggests that capitalist interests in the integrity of a given national economy have declined rather than advanced, and the recent macroeconomic policies of most advanced capitalist states strongly confirm this intuition. The abandonment of investment and price controls throughout the metropolitan capitalist world, the anarchic coming of a flexible exchange rate regime, and the related explosion in international currency movements all signal an era far different from the state monopoly capitalist school's presumptions. Rather than viewing separate national political processes as fundamentally involved in the imperialist protection of national capitalists from the vagaries of the world economy (the classic Leninist presumption), metropolitan state politics is actually more concerned with success-fully inserting the national economy into the internationalization process. In this context, a government is successful if its policies promote the importation and exportation of domestic *and* foreign capital.

This alternative to state monopoly capitalism has two advantages. In the first place, its focus on the global economy permits a more adequate analysis of post-war international organizations, especially the International Monetary Fund. The second advantage springs from the first. It is important to recognize that metropolitan imperialism cannot always be explained through an analysis of the policies of the major advanced capitalist nation-states. Depending on the circumstances, other institutions may play a much more active role in regulating the subordinated periphery or in coercing imperial antagonists. The rupture between capital centralization and nation-state authority demands this more flexible methodological approach.

The internationalizing process I have outlined should not be interpreted as causing an inexorable decline in the domestic power of the nation-state. In fact, pressures on any government to reorganize industry and discipline labor may be even greater than during an era of "liberal corporatism." Moreover, politicians and bureaucrats still must respond to discordant popular demands for economic regulation and security. Governments' attempts to soften capitalism's contradictions have often been interpreted by the state monopoly capital and world systems schools as the effort to construct a metropolitan national interest in economic expansionism and Third World exploitation. A more adequate interpretation would see the relevant political agents as responding to social pressures for capital's regulation within the constraints of promoting a region's ability to adapt to the demands of the world economy.

This structural/capital-logic synthesis (which both Fine and Harris [65] and Jessup [99] suggest in their works) represents an advance over the state monopoly capitalist school because it takes account of presently evolving global economic processes. It thereby frees us from the archaic pre-World War II premise of national capitalist centralization. This advantage is not unique to the approach I have outlined. The dependency world systems schools also emphasize the importance of analyzing the international structures of accumulation. On the other hand, I hope to demonstrate in the next section that the national capitalisms which have emerged in the periphery deserve an analysis different from the world systems dependency framework—one which is more sensitive to the variety of political processes which can integrate the Third World into the world capitalist system.

Capital penetration and the rise of the peripheral state
The explosion of Third World liberation movements and the subsequent formation of post-colonial states throughout Asia and Africa have attracted the interest of Marxist and non-Marxist social scientists alike. And most theorists have begun their academic explorations of these processes by examining the contradictions that arise between capitalist and precapitalist mechanisms of social reproduction.[33] This approach presents obvious difficulties for any

---

[33] Non-Marxist schools of thought often do not use this terminology, but a dichotomy is still drawn between "traditional" and "modern" societies.

theorist hoping to develop a general theory of Third World state formation. Given the variety of pre-capitalist political-economic forms of social organization, it would be unreasonable to expect the emergence of one type of peripheral state. Indeed, we have already noted that in certain regions (North America and parts of Oceania), where international commercial exchange was associated with the nearly complete elimination of indigenous peoples and large-scale human migration from the metropolis, capital penetration resulted in the eventual enlargement of the advanced capitalist world rather than the emergence of subordinated economic territories. For these reasons, analysts have long recognized the need to modify Marx's assertion that capital expansion must create a world after its own image.[34]

With this proviso in mind, it is important to recognize that there is more than a kernal of truth to The Communist Manifesto's buoyant claim. The internationalization of capital has not created a homogeneous capitalist world, but it has imposed a political-economic logic on the peripheral territories of the world economy. This is a key argument for any Marxist theory of imperialism. Certain structural features of the Third World state can be explained by considering abstractly the impact of capital penetration on a pre-capitalist society. In fact, without this general framework, the distinct particularities of a subordinated social formation's history and politics are impossible to decipher.

A schematic "historical" account best captures the key common features in the evolution of contemporary Third World states.[35]

1) Capital penetration initially results in the introduction of new social forms of production and exchange without this process necessarily dissolving the old. The array of modes of production within a territory thus becomes more complex.

2) Political institutions and practices must eventually emerge to preserve this unstable social arrangement if capital expansion is to continue. This, however, does not necessarily imply that the state

---

[34] The Manifesto actually contains a quite complex vision of capitalist evolution. The bourgeoisie "creates a world after its own image" but it also makes "barbarian and semi-barbarian countries dependent on the civilized ones, nations of peasants on nations of bourgeois, the East on the West." See [130, p. 477].

[35] Much of this analysis is stimulated by John G. Taylor's work in [175].

always acts to facilitate accumulation. It may be that contradictory social pressures prevent the pursuit of "rational" pro-bourgeois policies.

3) The commercialization of economic life and the concomitant attempt to extend new forms of political authority eventually give rise to what Marxists often label the petty-bourgeois intelligentsia (and what non-Marxists might call the modernizing elite). The proper name is not so important.[36] Rather, it is the key role which this non-bourgeois grouping plays in the creation of the peripheral state. Placed at the center of competing demands of metropolitan capital, a growing native bourgeoisie, a pre-capitalist oligarchy (which may or may not be merging with the bourgeoisie) and increasingly articulate laboring classes (the proletariat and the peasantry), the actions of the intelligentsia are central to Third World political struggle.

4) The rise of this new class parallels the key role which the peripheral state plays in the organization of the territory's economic life. This often implies the backing of infra-structural building projects and the creation of certain state capitalist enterprises.

5) Even more fundamental is the introduction of a "modern" repressive apparatus that is able to monitor and control the actions of the popular classes. Because of this imperative, military institutions become central to the integrity of most peripheral social formations. The spread of capitalist social relations is integrally connected to the flourishing of nationally-based military institutions.[37]

6) All of these developments point to the emergence of distinct nationalities as a reference point for political action. Coincident with the rise of literacy, nationalist activists draw on metaphors and

---

[36] The name that one gives to a social grouping can be important. Terminology normally betrays a complex set of theoretical presumptions about historical evolution. Nevertheless, nearly all social analysts agree that the "new petty bourgeoisie" or "modernizing elite" are central to the revolutionary transitions of the "capitalist," "socialist" or "modern" world. For an orthodox, sociological view, see [53]. John S. Saul provides an excellent summary of Marxist views on the "new middle class" in [162]. Few deny the importance of this social grouping, but there is a vigorous debate about its "progressive" historical role.

[37] For a controversial, non-Marxist account of the military's central role in Third World state formation, see Irving Louis Horowitz in [93, pp. 89–186].

key cultural symbols to separate the indigenous society from the imperial one, while simultaneously appropriating some core practices and ideologies that permit the legitimation of capitalist nation-state practices.[38]

7) The creation of a new nationalist ideology has its parallel in the attempt by leaders of a Third World state to reorganize its economic relations with the surrounding regional and world economy. This can take many different forms, but the instability of global capitalism constantly reproduces the need for peripheral state action. Relations between center and periphery thus are chronically problematic.

This schematic accounting of peripheral state formation has drawn implicitly on a key concept developed by Marxist theorists in the early twentieth century. Trotsky used the term "combined and uneven development" and "permanent revolution" both to analyze the sources of social instability in the Tsarist state and to argue for the possibility of socialist revolution. He maintained that capital penetration inevitably produces economic, political and ideological anomalies that the pre-capitalist state proves increasingly unable to manage. Moreover, the weakness of indigenous capitalist interests (as a result of imperial domination) can combine with the proletarianization of the national economy to generate a powerful socialist revolutionary movement. Trotsky and Lenin linked this vision of successful socialist revolution in Russia to the spread of proletarian upheaval in the more advanced West. They did not forsee the stabilization of an anti-imperialist regime without such a development.[39]

It is necessary to modify Trotsky's argument to account for certain historical developments that are now, in the late twentieth century, much easier to discern. In the first place: anti-imperialist, national revolutions have resulted in the establishment of more politically autonomous peripheral states without socialist revolution in the West. The rise of the Soviet Union is the clearest early example of this process, but one should also interpret the formation

---

[38] Benedict Anderson is one of the few to have grappled directly with the theoretical complexities of this phenomenon. (See [10].)

[39] Michael Loewy in [119] presents an insightful commentary on the history of the term *permanent revolution*.

of the Turkish and Mexican states during the early twentieth
century within the same general framework.[40] More recently, events
in Nicaragua and Iran confirm the power of this modified combined
and uneven development hypothesis: imperial capital penetration
generates intense destabilizing pressures against a compradore
imperial regime. The heterogeneous political structures that correspond to the initial states of capital penetration become increasingly difficult to maintain, but the new states which do emerge in
the aftermath of revolution or intense reformist pressures must
survive in a capitalist world economy. Their successes do not signal
the disintegration of global capitalism.

This last point leads to a second crucial modification to Trotsky's
analysis: an abstract consideration of the political effects of combined and uneven development cannot account for the variety of
recent historical experiences in Third World social formations. The
character of economic contradictions facing a society, the global
political economic context of imperial domination and the actual
evolution of peripheral political structures all interact to shape the
oppositional political traditions and programs of a peripheral
society. The very different post-colonial experiences of the Ivory
Coast and Ghana, or the sharp distinction between the post-
revolutionary Iranian and Nicaraguan regimes cannot be explained
without a more historically sensitive attention to details.

A Marxist theory of peripheral state formation cannot deduce all
political processes from the impacts of capital penetration.
Nevertheless, it is important to recognize that there already is a
framework embedded within the combined and uneven development model that can help explain variations across space and time.
The implicit message of this analysis is that the peripheral state
emerges from an interaction of imperialist state actions, the
demands of metropolitan capitals, the complex processes of resistance and collaboration among Third World economic elites, and
the similar dynamic that takes place within the indigenous governing institutions of the periphery. This approach does not neglect the
actions of the subordinated classes, for all governing authorities
must attempt to channel or repress the political energies of outcaste

---

[40] Trotsky himself implicitly recognized this perspective in his analysis of Mexico.
See [119, p. 92].

groups. Nevertheless, a focus on the elites is especially important if we are to understand the political-economic reproduction of a Third World World social order. A stable "quadruple alliance" among the political and economic elites in the periphery and center is a prerequisite for the security of most Third World states.[41]

In this approach, there is wide scope for a variety of political structures within the Third World. Parliamentary democracy can become consolidated in certain nations, while military dictatorship remains chronic in other neighboring states. The terms of imperial subordination can also differ—from a framework in which local capital and the Third World state have very little room for negotiation (Puerto Rico) to one in which the Third World state and local capital possess a surprising ability to direct the terms of metropolitan capital penetration, even if, in military and diplomatic terms, these local elites are firmly dependent on metropolitan imperial powers (South Korea). This analysis also suggests that the terms of the "quadruple alliance" can also change over time. The evolution of the Brazilian state during the 1970s and 1980s is an important case in point.

This analysis has taken us a long way from Marx's simplistic claim that capital penetration must create a homogeneous capitalist world. But, in another sense, we are not that distanced from his and Engels' mid-19th century intuitions. The *Communist Manifesto* prediction was incorrect. On the other hand, the emphasis on the need to analyze peripheral state formation in the context of international capital penetration remains valid. It is for this reason that the early twentieth century combined and uneven framework is still cogent today.

Conclusion

These dual discussions of metropolitan and peripheral state forma- tion are unified in their attempts to trace the recent evolution of political structures and capabilities to the internationalization of capital. In the case of the advanced capitalist social formation, I argued that the explosive interpenetration of capitals has generated new "a-national" regulatory structures and thereby lessened the

---

[41] The term "quadruple alliance" is a modification of Evans' "triple alliance" formulation in [41].

plausibility of state monopoly capitalist analysis. Indeed, the new advanced capitalist nation-state's integrity depends on the relatively effective functioning of these transnational mechanisms, not on the perfection of centralized mechanisms of control within the nation-state.

This discovery of the importance of world economic processes in metropolitan nation-state formation is not new. On the other hand, the virulence of nationalist and capitalist imperialist conflict in the early twentieth century led to the articulation of a particularly compelling theoretical vision that links uneven development to imperialist war. The contemporary obsolescence of this framework forces us to reformulate the nation-state/capital internationalization dialectic.

This theoretical uncertainty does not exist in the same degree for analyses of the Third World state. Few would argue that this entity is solely formed by national forces, and most Marxists—either consciously or unconsciously—have continued to use the combined and uneven development model to explain the "peculiar" nationalist/internationalist mixtures in the state structures and political cultures of the Third World. The difficulty with this theoretical borrowing lies not in the actual skeleton of the argument, but rather its sometimes too ambitious application.

For example, the effort to explain the inevitability of successful anti-imperialist revolution neglects the symbiotic alliances that normally emerge between peripheral and metropolitan states and capitals, and the attempts to deduce a single authoritarian structure of political dominance fail to account for the immense chronological and cross-sectional variety in Third World politics. In both of these cases, there is a tendency to neglect those particular "quadruple alliances" which influence the trajectory of any given social formation. Wallerstein in [186], for example, attempts to trace all shifts in political fortunes to the secular, long-wave rhythms in accumulation. It should be obvious by now that this approach claims too much for economic forces. The Marxist analysis of global accumulation provides a basis for understanding the processes of state formation; it cannot abolish the study of political and cultural processes altogether.

Making this argument need not indicate a significant modification of Leninist theory—if it could be shown that the peripheral states' own actions are a straightforward result of capital expansion. Unfortunately, this is not the case. The combined and uneven development perspective can be used to anticipate the emergence of bureaucratic and repressive peripheral states that often dominate local bourgeois interests and sometimes clash with advanced capitalist state demands. On the other hand, we cannot predict the precise political configurations that emerge from this process without doing considerable violence to history. As E. P. Thompson noted in [176, p. 343].

Do the categories of "class struggle on a world scale" really explain to us the course of the Iranian revolution? The degeneration of the regime of Pol Pot? The adversary relations of China and the USSR? The generational shifts in political consciousness in Europe, East and West, associated with the peace movement and the movement for civil rights? Or the imperial atavism of the British government's response to the Falklands crisis? By attempting to explain it all in one global mouthful we end with everything left to be explained.

The indeterminancy in this metropolitan and Third World state analysis can be traced to the same source. Neither imperial nor subordinate state behavior can be explained without reference to more specific national and international historical processes.

No narrow focus on the tendencies of capital can by itself explain state behavior. The method does account for certain general structural trends in the evolution of the global polity, but these findings only provide a basis for understanding the subject of imperialism proper. It is still necessary to develop a framework that can model the interactions among core and peripheral nation-states and international organizations. Otherwise, it will not be possible to anticipate the shifting contours of political-economic subordination and conflict so basic to the capitalist world.

C. Explaining capitalist imperial oppression

Introduction: Why imperialism? The Liberal challenge
It is always tempting to argue that contemporary political and economic structures of the capitalist world economy are the direct expression of an unfolding logic in capital expansion. The arguments of the preceding two sections, however, need not evoke this ineluctable magic. The strikingly different pattern of post-war capital internationalization is a result of an advanced capitalist

political settlement after World War II, which itself was formed by three qualitatively new developments: the hegemonic position of the United States, the emergence of the Soviet Union as a major world power and the intensifying strength of national liberation and anticolonial struggles in the periphery.

As Figure 2 suggests, in order to discuss the impact of capital expansion on metropolitan and peripheral state formation in the modern period (A), it was necessary to presume a knowledge of the general political framework of the economy (B, C, D, and E). If we had remained at this most general theoretical level, it would not have been possible to reach any general findings. Starting with capital expansion presupposes a necessary, but arbitrary, theoretical entry into an interconnected process.

This methodological conclusion poses a strong challenge to the Marxist theory of imperialism. If capitalist state structures and political practices are only indirectly regulated by accumulation dynamics, then in what sense can it be argued that imperialism is an essential part of capitalism? A skeptical answer to this straightforward question is the basis of most liberal rejections of radical theory. Instead, it is claimed that imperialism is a result of unique historically-based factors which presumably can be expurgated from the body politic by an enlightened citizenry.

It is the central task of this section to answer this challenge. The key claim will be that the undeniable presence of metropolitan economic interests in peripheral territories has combined with powerful political tendencies within the center and periphery to sustain and even strengthen the practices of capitalist imperialist coercion. In the abstract, this oppression is not necessary for the maintenance of capitalism; in the sphere of historical reality, the capitalist organization of material life and imperialism cannot be decoupled.

In arguing for this materialist perspective, it is important to acknowledge that a key aspect of the liberal criticism is granted. Marxists have often incorrectly maintained that metropolitan capital survives on constant transfusions of economic surplus that are coerced from the periphery. This parasitism argument was a central aspect of the early Comintern's analysis of capitalist evolution, and it still plays a key role in many post-World War II theoretical and rhetorical formulations. For this reason, it is first necessary to dispose of this argument. Understanding why capitalist imperialism is *not* an *economic* inevitability is key to determining why imperialist coercion and conflict are such inevitable features of the capitalist global economy.

Post-Leninist theories of economic parasitism

The focus on economic exploitation and parasitism has acquired a more sophisticated theoretical and empirical apparatus since the World War I period, but it would be incorrect to suggest that one single radical paradigm predominates. One school has placed special emphasis on surplus value extraction through trade (unequal exchange); another places more weight on the institutional regulation of primary product pricing; a third argues for the emergence of a multinational-directed international division of labor; while a fourth attempts to document Hobson's and Lenin's original stress on debilitating financial surplus extraction. None of these perspectives are at all mutually exclusive; in fact they all suffer from similar theoretical weaknesses. Nevertheless, it is useful to examine each hypothesis separately.

Institutionalized Exploitation Through Trade: The Unequal Exchange Model.

The assertion that international exchange itself is exploitative marks an important departure from traditional Marxian theory.[42] In volume I of *Capital*, exploitation is viewed as the appropriation of surplus value generated by the "extra" productive labor of wage workers—where value is defined as the socially necessary abstract labor time associated with the production of a given commodity.[43] World systems and unequal exchange theorists dispute this assertion. In his seminal statement on unequal exchange, Arghiri

---

[42] Note that Marx stressed the non-exploitative character of trade in [126, p. 258]: The sphere of circulation or commodity exchange, within whose boundaries the sale and purchase of labor-power goes on, is in fact a very Eden of the innate rights of man. It is the exclusive realm of Freedom, Equality, Property and Bentham.

[43] This is the standard definition of value, but, as shall be seen, the unequal exchange debate revolves around the quantification of *abstract* labor time. For this discussion to have any meaning, it must be supposed that value does have a quantitative dimension—even if the determination of this "quantity" depends on the act of exchange. For the seminal, qualitatively-oriented discussion of this issue, see I. I. Rubin in [159].

Emmanuel maintains in [54] that there are two mechanisms within the social accounting rules of capitalism that facilitate a transfer of value from one capitalist sector to another. Marx himself demonstrates (although in an inadequate fashion) that those sectors with a relatively high "organic composition of capital" receive additional surplus value through trade with low "organic composition of capital" sectors. In developing this point, Marx assumes a national social formation characterized by free capital mobility and a customary social subsistence wage for all workers. In other words, he assumes a tendency for both profit and wage rates to equalize.

Emmanuel notes these dual assumptions and then argues that it would be more realistic to assume capital mobility and labor immobility. He accurately notes that wage differentials within the world economy are enormous, while there is a rough equality among profit rates. If Emmanuel's assumptions are adopted, then it can be shown through similar reasoning to Marx's that the profit rate equalization process will result in a transfer of value to the high wage sector—since both low wage and high wage workers are assumed in this model to produce roughly the same amount of value in any working day, and yet prices in the low wage area will be lower because capital costs are lower. In this analysis, it is crucial to assume that all countries have access to the same technology.[44]

Despite the logical plausibility of this argument, there is reason to question Emmanuel's analysis. Does trade between high wage and low wage sectors really represent exploitation or unequal exchange? Many have argued that this thesis rests on a misunderstanding of Marxian value theory.[45] According to this perspective, all commodites within any given sector of production must have the same value (the same socially necessary abstract labor embedded within them). Otherwise, one would have to dismiss the law of value—the thesis that capital carries with it a coercive logic forcing production to correspond to the value relations associated with generalized

---

[44] John Roemer recently provided a generalization of Emmanuel's argument in [158]. He demonstrated that a country experiences unequal exchange if it imports capital and/or exports labor.

[45] The following argument rests heavily on Alain de Janvry and Frank Kramer's analysis in [46]. Although resting on different methodological foundations, a similar critique of unequal exchange has recently been presented by Susan Himmelweit in [90].

commodity exchange. This implies that there can be no unequal exchange associated with the trade of non-specific commodities; that is, goods which can be produced in both high-wage and low-wage sectors of the world economy. Further, if we assume capital mobility (as does Emmanuel), wages in the non-specific production sectors will correspond to differential labor productivities. Otherwise, production would be only located in that sector where wages were lower relative to labor productivity.[46] These points reduce the unequal exchange argument to a consideration of the trade of specific commodities—goods which for geographical and historical reasons can only be produced in a defined region of the globe.

Even in this case, it can plausibly be argued that the transfer of value which Emmanuel asserts to be exploitative is a further misinterpretation of Marxian theory. The key to determining whether or not an economic process (either in the sphere of exchange or production) is exploitative depends on a conceptualization of less coercive social relations (or property distributions) which allow the particular practice (or result) to be eliminated.[47] In the case of Marx's focus on the labor process and wage labor, it is possible to construct an alternative social arrangement which eliminates the coercive value relations that are basic to capitalism. It is more difficult to maintain in a similar way that the *pure* pricing mechanism of capitalism is exploitative. In any complex society in which market relations are still important, prices most probably would reflect the cost of tying up resources in fixed means of production. Moreover, to the extent that wage differentials remain, prices of the final products should bear some relation to wage costs. It is not the price formation process which is exploitative in capitalism, but the capital-labor relation that lies behind it.

Ernest Mandel and Charles Bettelheim agree with this last criticism in [124] and [54] and thus maintain that Emmanuel should have attempted to explain the wage differentials between the core and periphery rather than treating these variables as exogenous to the dynamics of accumulation. For Mandel, in particular, unequal exchange is caused by the differential development of labor

---

[46] Note that this analysis abstracts from transportation costs.

[47] John Roemer provides a concise explanation of this approach in [157].

productivities throughout the world economy. While this formulation fits more easily into the confines of Marxist value theory, it, for
this reason, fails to demonstrate that trade leads to the extraction of
value from low wage to high wage sectors. Mandel is thus unable to
prove that metropolitan capital receives a boost from the unequal
exchange mechanisms that he hypothesizes. This particular post-war
theoretical development has reached a dead end.

A deterioration in the terms of trade?

One alternative to the unequal exchange thesis also attempts to
unearth an inherently exploitative mechanism in metropolitan/
periphery trade. This structuralist approach, however, does not rely
on the obscurities of value theory. Rather, the deterioration in the
Third World terms of trade is explained by positing unequal power
relations in the world economy.

Raul Prebisch first articulated this approach in the early 1950s in
[148]. During times of prosperity, both workers and capitalists in
the advanced capitalist countries are able to raise their wages and
prices relative to those of the Third World; while, during recessions,
primary product prices actually deteriorate in absolute terms while
those of manufactured goods stabilize. This framework crucially
depends on the argument that the economic agents of advanced
capitalist countries possess greater economic power during all
phases of the world economy; it predicts a continuing deterioration
of the terms of trade. The radical version of this thesis does not
really take issue with Prebisch's hypothesized mechanisms. Rather,
dependency and world systems theorists note that ready access to
cheap raw materials permits the consolidation of the imperialist
welfare state.

With respect to the terms of trade between manufactured and
primary commodities, the empirical evidence for the structuralist
claim is strong during most periods of the post-war epoch. The
World Bank reports in [195, p. 11] that from the Korean War until
the early 1970s, the relative prices of raw materials slumped. During
the OPEC crisis of 1973–4, this trend was sharply reversed for
nearly all raw material exports; moreover, in 1979, petroleum prices
again rose sharply. Nevertheless, by the early 1980s, the terms of
trade for primary commodities had again deteriorated. A Prebisch
supporter could claim that the underlying trend predicted by this

model has been verified. Indeed, because structuralists drew the policy conclusion that only the formation of raw material cartels could reverse the deterioration in relative Third World export prices, one could reasonably argue that the OPEC experience was the exception to commodity price movements that proved the rule.[48]

There is, however, an important anomaly in this prediction. A major result of the international trading dynamic was presumed to be the lack of economic diversification within the Third World economies. This dependence on one or two primary commodities does remain true for most of Africa and certain Latin American countries. On the other hand, other national economies of South America and a series of East Asian countries experienced an impressive industrialization during the 1970s.[49] Despite the relatively poor performance of the traditional exports of the less developed territories, other mechanisms have been at work to reorganize the international structure of production. Indeed, it is striking that (with the important exception of Mexico) those countries which have experienced the most dramatic industrial transformation of their economies are petroleum product importers. Undoubtedly, the determination of primary product prices plays an important role in regulating the accumulation prospects of many social formations, but the dynamics of raw material/manufactured trade between North and South cannot explain the evolving structure of the world economy. Nor is there a necessary correspondence between the reality of this dynamic and the general material interests of metropolitan capital.

A new international division of labor?

The failure to anticipate the changing organization of international trade has led to a general reconsideration of the possible dynamics of international exploitation. As a result, new theories have been articulated which focus on the establishment of productive enterprises under the control of Northern capital. A greater number of Marxist theorists are now suggesting that this process has

---

[48] This was certainly the basis for the UNCTAD program for the formation of producers commodity associations, as outlined in [181, 134–54].

[49] See [196] for information on the development prospects of the Third World.

established a new international division of labor allowing metropolitan capital to intensify the rate of exploitation over all wage workers. Raw material/manufactured trade has been replaced by out-sourcing and the proliferation of assembly operations in low-wage, "platform" regions of the Third World.[50]

To the extent that this posited tendency is an accurate description of present trends, this analysis also suggests an important change in the material interests that citizens of a metropolitan social formation might have in maintaining contemporary imperial structures of accumulation. In the short run, certain sectors of the industrial proletariat will oppose the diversification of the world economy, and to the extent that the new productive enterprises of the Third World also breed worker resistance, it might be possible to hypothesize an internationalist upswelling of resistance to the rule of capital. On the other hand, a longer-run perspective could lead to less sanguine conclusions. Industrial displacement could eventually culminate in the establishment of "clean" service jobs that monitor and regulate production in the Third World. Metropolitan workers may acquire an even more direct interest in the maintenance of the global economy, since the peoples of the "tropics" could come to labor at subsistence wages directly under their supervision. Hobson in warning against this possibility [92] may have erred only in being premature.

The new international division of labor hypothesis (NIDL) is intimately linked to two empirical claims: (1) that transnational corporations are progressively establishing their grip over all sectors of the capitalist world economy, and (2) that subsidiaries established in the Third World primarily exist to service metropolitan needs. This latter argument bears a close relationship to the earlier structuralist hypothesis that metropolitan capital forces the Third World to produce raw materials for metropolitan consumption. With respect to the first point, there is no doubt that transnational

---

[50] Froebel, Heinrich, and Kaye [74, p. 403] state this perspective most sharply: Although a new international division of labor has been brought into existence by the new and increasingly dominant process of the world market oriented industrialization of these countries, this form of industrialization has not meant any change in the historical process of underdevelopment but in fact in its deepening.

For a critique of this perspective as well as the presentation of useful statistical data that warns us against over-stressing the general industrialization tendency in all of the Third World, see Rhys Jenkins' analysis in [98].

corporate activity is entering into new fields of accumulation in both the metropolitan and Third World. The earlier discussion of the internationalization of capital strongly supports this argument. On the other hand, it is also true that the Third World state and even some Third World capitalist combines have come to play an important role in the regulation of certain productive enterprises. Co-partnership agreements and employee training pacts are now a common feature of much transnational activity.

Peter Evans, in an important study of Brazilian state capitalism [57], argues that the state does attempt to force metropolitan capital to divest itself of control in certain mature industries which no longer possess the most advanced technology. On the other hand, in those sectors where local capital has little ability to compete either domestically or internationally, management remains firmly in the hands of Northern corporate headquarters. Given the heavy involvement of the state in the economic organization of most Newly Industrialized Countries, Evans' findings can be generalized. Charles Barone, for instance, stresses the important influence of the South Korean government in regulating (within the constraints already noted) multinational and domestic capitalist behavior [21].

This modification of the first aspect of the New International Division of Labor hypothesis would not really be relevant if the second claim of this perspective could be sustained: that global production and trade is organized to service the needs of metropolitan social formations, while those of the Third World are ignored. Is it true that capitalist production in the periphery is mainly outward-oriented?

Throughout the 1970s, this was not uniformly the case. Per-capita domestic consumption levels rose relatively rapidly in most Third World countries. Moreover, high rates of growth in internal production were strongly linked to intensified inward flows of metropolitan capital.[51] Note that it is not being claimed that the

---

[51] Between 1974 and 1978, the East Asian and Latin American/Caribbean LDCs imported an average of $28 billion dollars of capital per year. This represented 78% of all capital flowing to oil-importing LDCs. More significantly, the much smaller sample of high-income LDCs (grouped in East Asia and Latin America imported $19 billion annually, or 53% of total capital imports to oil-importing LDCs. For more data on this experience, see [141].

peasants and workers of these previously expanding Third World countries necessarily enjoyed improved living standards. In certain important cases (such as Brazil) the absolute consumption and income levels of low income citizens stagnated or declined over the 1960s and 1970s. On the other hand, this period of rapid growth did permit the substantial enrichment of a considerable Third World professional and managerial class.[52]

The return of financial parasitism?
If the 1970s experience does not provide strong support for the NIDL perspective, the 1980s debt crisis does appear to buttress this neo-dependency thesis. The IMF austerity programs that Brazil and Mexico have accepted, for instance, are specifically designed to immiserate all sectors of the domestic economy in order to increase the relative share of production that services the export market. At the same time, these states are under pressure to moderate their controls over foreign investment and thereby encourage the increased penetration of metropolitan capital. There is clearly a logic at work which links the continued expansion of international capital to the subordination of Third World productive effort—both in terms of the direct macroeconomic control over Third World policy management and in terms of an intensified "servicing" of the metropolitan market. In other words, the instability of international capitalism during the 1970s seems to have culminated in a process that closely corresponds to the perspectives that have just been rejected. The Leninist financial parasitism thesis appears much more prescient.

Before concluding, however, that the deep capitalist slump has created subservient and stagnant economic appendages throughout the Third World, it is important to note that the impact of metropolitan capitalist stagnation has not been uniform. Most East Asian countries, for instance, have maintained surprisingly stable financial relations with the advanced capitalist world. In fact, their debt-service ratios (with respect to exports) remain well under twenty percent, while many major South American and African nations are experiencing interest and principal payment demands that are well above that level. It is true that 1983 represented the

---

[52] For a debate on these issues see Fishlow and Fields in [66] and [64] respectively.

first year since 1966 that the GDP rate of growth for developing countries fell below the advanced capitalist world's. (See [196, p. 12].) But past history suggests that this trend will continue only if stagnation in the total world economy persists. The general instabilities of global capitalism may doom much of the Third World, but, in this case, the advanced capitalist nations will also experience chronic economic difficulties. Certainly, the relative social pain cannot be compared; the prospect of permanent stagnation for the periphery is disastrous. The theoretical point, however, is that the parasitism analysis cannot coherently explain the booms and slumps of the world economy, nor can it discern the economic differentiation of the periphery that has continued through all phases of the global business cycle.

The four hypotheses we considered all posit somewhat different realities. On the other hand, they are all unified in presuming that particular exploitative mechanisms doom the Third World to stagnation and subservience. It is this monolithic vision which reveals the inadequacy of these radical theories. They simply cannot allow for the variability in the political economic trajectories of different sectors of the Third World.

This inadequacy is unfortunate. By claiming too much for the power of purely economic mechanisms, the rhetoric blinds the skeptical reader to more prosaic economic realities. It is not necessary to claim that imperial exploitation is associated with an always unequal and subordinated international division of labor. The evolution of capitalism has never yet been characterized by a stabilized distribution of productive activities, and new centers of accumulation have regularly emerged throughout the nineteenth and twentieth centuries. On the other hand, the export of money and productive capital does necessarily establish metropolitan claims on the future productive effort of the periphery. And, as Hobson and Lenin note, these claims could conceivably lead to the development of a nation in which there is a strong bourgeois interest in maintaining the already existent circuits of accumulation.

This argument does not rely on the notion that metropolitan-peripheral economic relations are *uniquely* exploitative. Sectors of metropolitan capital do extract surplus from peripheral workers by directly setting their labor in motion within subsidiary enterprises and by appropriating a portion of the surplus product in the form of interest and dividend payments. These processes, however, are also familiar to the advanced capitalist world. Many advanced capitalist workers labor for foreign subsidiaries, and the present U.S. dependence on short-term capital flows for the financing of its trade and budgetary deficits could, in another context, easily be interpreted as typical of an unstable Third World country. For this reason, it is difficult to use the structure of capital flow patterns to differentiate advanced capitalist from peripheral social formations.

In this discussion, I have rejected a key premise in many Marxist theories of imperialism. It is not true that global capitalism must coerce the Third World into a position of permanent economic backwardness. This conclusion is at sharp variance with much radical work on this subject, but recognizing its validity is essential for the development of a more adequate theory of imperialism. *On the level of the abstract theory of capital expansion and exploitation,* it is not possible to argue for the inevitable necessity of the North-South divide.

Towards an alternative materialist framework: Conceptualizing imperialist oppression and its mechanisms
A theory of imperialism must, above all, identify and account for mechanisms of territorial and/or national subordination. An abstract definition of this form of oppression has two dimensions. A nation experiences political-economic domination if: (1) its political and economic life is largely determined and regulated by decisions and forces subject to the control of foreign, non-indigenous interests; and (2) its own politics and culture regularly resist basic aspects of this dependence. This latter aspect of imperial oppression is less familiar, but is in fact more crucial to a proper understanding of this phenomenon.

Canada's economy, for instance, is thoroughly subject to US control: an extremely high percentage of its foreign assets are owned by US nationals and its macroeconomic health largely depends on favorable conditions of accumulation within the US. On the other hand, Canada is also an important member of NATO and plays a significant role in political-economic negotiations among the Northern capitalist powers. Because its polity is relatively unproblematically integrated into this imperial apparatus, it cannot be claimed that Canada is an oppressed peripheral social formation.

On the other hand, Argentina's economy is subject to more national ownership than Canada's.[53] In addition, its crucial agricultural exports are partly regulated by the Soviet Union's demand for grain. These economic facts, however, do not mean that Argentina is subject to less coercive foreign direction. On the contrary, Argentina's peripheral status is due to the *incomplete* material and cultural integration of its politics into imperial structures.[54] Because Argentina's political struggles regularly focus on the legitimacy of metropolitan capitalist interests, external institutions are more likely to intervene forcefully to regulate the nation's domestic political fortunes. Economic dependence on the global capitalist economy is a necessary condition for the exercise of imperial power. Otherwise, there would be little incentive for the implementation of oppressive measures. Nevertheless, this factor does not by itself permit a differentiation of the world's polities. Every social formation within the world economy has interests in others. More important in distinguishing the center from periphery is identifying the separate processes of class formation that underlie the exercise of global imperialist politics.

This framework has the advantage of allowing the anticipation of changing patterns of imperial subordination. If shifting conditions of accumulation helped to create a Canadian mass movement agitating for a disengagement from imperial structures and the establishment of new, anticapitalist mechanisms of regulation, this would undoubtedly stimulate a US imperial intervention. Canada could become transformed into a peripheral social formation by this political process. In other words, the emergence of a mass-based anti-imperialist politics could lead the Canadian social formation to have more in common with Argentina than its present NATO allies.

Another example that may be illuminating is the case of Puerto Rico. Gordon Lewis has noted in [116] that no nation in the Caribbean has been more thoroughly integrated into the U.S. polity and economy, and yet this fusion is not complete. Puerto Rican

---

[53] See [183] for some comparative, if dated, data.
[54] This perspective seems far different from Franz Fanon's emphasis on cultural imperialism in [59]. Nevertheless I would view his works as a powerful text expressing the problematic ideological nature of Western capital penetration. A more precise articulation of this problematic can be found in analysis Albert Memmi's in [133].

culture and politics have regularly produced oppositional currents that promote the disengagement of this island society from U.S. capitalism. At the same time, the massive movement of Puerto Ricans to and from the United States, the participation of its young adults in the American armed forces, the huge transfer payments to the island all create an alternative politics and culture that evoke the "hope" of complete integration. In this case, the dream is to overcome imperial subordination by joining the imperialist power. This is a possible, if not likely, development for Puerto Rico. Just as Canada might find itself disengaged from and subordinated to the United States, the peoples of other nations may participate in the construction of political/cultural processes that render the term *imperialism* irrelevant as an analytic description of a particular international relation.

The potential political-economic malleability in the core-periphery distinction has its counterpart in the wide array of international policies that reinforce metropolitan control. In times of relative stability, "normal" diplomacy predominates. Political support is traded for subsidized assistance, programs that encourage capital penetration and the forging of closer links among state and quasi-state bodies. Military assistance, bilateral foreign aid, training in educational institutions, government-sponsored trade union communications, and some international aid programs all fall within this category. It is the utopian goal of metropolitan diplomacy to forge such effective programs of this type that there will never be any need to initiate "dirtier" practices of coercion. In a sense, the task of these policies is to eliminate the need for imperial oppression altogether, thereby eliminating the core-periphery distinction.

This liberal attempt to banish the need for imperialism is illusory. Nevertheless, the dream of capitalist peace does provide the basis for conflicts within the imperial state. When economic conditions deteriorate, the developmental goals of some aid programs conflict with the demands of international capital for increased direct control over production and circulation. When social "disruptions" intensify, attempts to strengthen the repressive apparatus seriously strain ties with social institutions (labor unions, universities, peasant organizations) that were formerly seen as fundamental to political-economic stability. In the most extreme cases, imperial-sponsored counter-insurgency war destroys all attempt to construct a stable, liberal capitalist form of regulation.

There is, however, a larger unity behind this liberal/conservative conflict. As long as imperial control is basic to the reproduction of global capitalism (in a historical sense), the effectiveness of "liberal" intervention depends on its reversibility. Economic aid and capital penetration should integrate an economy so that international destabilization is possible. The sponsoring of social reforms should divide political coalitions so that repression can be systematically directed towards the elimination of more intransigent opposition. The sharp conflicts that sometimes arise within the imperial state should not mask the essential continuity that runs between advanced capitalist economic and military interventions.[55]

It should be clear that this conceptualization of the instruments of imperial oppression is predicted on the assumption that the more "extreme" practices of domination are fundamental to the organization of contemporary global capitalism. Otherwise, one could interpret foreign assistance and programs of institutional cooperation between metropolitan and peripheral states as anti-imperialist initiatives. Because these programs do anticipate the creation of friendly states through external manipulation, commentators such as Hayter [88] have argued that all granting of foreign aid is imperialistic. For our purposes, however, this approach is too broadly focussed. If *imperialism* is to have a precise meaning, it must imply systematic political-economic domination that ultimately rests on the use of coercive force. Making such a judgment requires a historical perspective that links shifting conditions of accumulation to the emergence and continuation of coercive global political relations.

Towards an alternative materialist framework: The historical logic of imperial oppression
A materially-based theory of imperialism need not prove that international coercion and conflict is optimally functional to global capitalism's reproduction. It is not even necessary to assume that the ultimate result of imperialist behavior is rational from the perspective of capital. On the other hand, such an approach does

---

[55] Louise FitzSimons reports in [67, pp. 173–214] that the Kennedy Administration had a particularly clear conception of the continuity running between foreign aid and counter-insurgency efforts. It pushed vigorously and successfully for both—although its dual commitment was never really tested by a breakdown in imperialist structures (as the Johnson Administration was shaken in Vietnam.)

require a step-by-step explanation which indicates how a series of
responses to certain inherent social contradictions can culminate in
the systematic expression of imperial politics. In this way, an analyst
can develop a general framework that is able to explain and
anticipate tendencies in political-economic behavior within and
among dominant and subordinate polities. In developing this
"historical" (as opposed to structural-functionalist) logic of imperialism, I will begin by drawing on the "economic-level" and
"political-level" conclusions of the preceding two sections.[56] This
method is subject to the earlier methodological warnings: beginning
with a study of economic contradictions does not imply that this
"base" exerts causal primacy (even in the last instance) over all
other forms of social action. Rather, this grounded approach more
easily permits the theoretical construction of the structure and
movement of imperialism's essential aspects.

Capital expansion and the differentiation of the world economy
The traditional beginning of most Marxian theories of imperialism is
still adequate: a fundamental aspect of capitalism as a mode of
organizing material life is its qualitatively more forceful expansive
power. Accumulation leads to the consolidation of capitalist social
relations within a home, national territory and the creation of new
production relations on the nation's commercial periphery. The
internal process does not come prior to the external. Rather, this
analysis suggests that the social and political differentiation of
territories is a fundamental feature of the beginnings of capital
expansion.[57]

These new forms of economic organization have immediate
political ramifications. On the one hand, the ruling classes of the
newly-created peripheral social formations must respond to the
intensified commercial demands on their social order. Compradore
merchants and landholders arise to raise demands for more autonomy and power. Resistance to these foreign and local bourgeois

---

[56] This concept is taken from E. P. Thompson [177]. On a more abstract level, I
have attempted to employ Anthony Giddens' theory of structuration—the non-
functionalist accounting of the reproduction of structures of domination through time
and space (or what Giddens calls *time-space distanciation*). This is outlined in [81].

[57] Wallerstein is the theorist best known for pursuing the implications of this
analysis. For a relatively abstract presentation of his method, see [187].

pressures is often prolonged, but the result of this process has normally been either the formation of political structures clearly subordinated to metropolitan capital,[58] or the creation of independent political orders that have the capability of "joining" the metropolitan world.

Peripheral state formation and the intensification of imperialist politics in the metropolitan world
The earlier discussion of peripheral state formation stressed the importance of studying "non-economic" factors. The construction of new national ideologies, the pivotal position of the "modernizing intelligentisia," the emergence of national military institutions were all interpreted as essential aspects of the capital penetration dynamic.

But what of the metropolitan world? It is inadequate to leave political and cultural analysis in the periphery, for capital export has a generalizing impact on metropolitan life as well. Marxists have occasionally addressed this issue, particularly in discussions of the aristocracy of labor. Nevertheless, the analysis has been quite scattered and incomplete. This is unfortunate. *Understanding the reasons for the emergence of an imperialist politics and culture within the advanced capitalist nation-state is key to uncovering the historical logic of imperialism.*

Resistance to capital expansion from the periphery has a profound effect on the metropolitan political order. Already emerging economic, diplomatic and military interests agitate for support against the external challenge, and complex ideologies supporting the moral need for national intervention into and control over external territories become popularly elaborated. The almost uniform success of modern imperialist ideology is poorly understood,[59] but I would argue that there are three material reasons (which do *not* depend on the argument that imperialist exploitation is essential to the viability of an advanced capitalist social formation) why

---

[58] Braudel notes in [30, p. 102] that:
It is only a step from market to colony. The exploited have only to cheat, or to protest, and conquest immediately follows.
[59] The most persuasive account of British imperial ideology can be found in Anthony Barnett's *Iron Britannica* [20]. William Appleman Williams has been the primary investigator of this issue in the US context. (See [191].)

metropolitan publics so often enthusiastically embrace the politics of international coercion. First the advanced capitalist state response to anti-imperialist struggles has often been successful, and the consequent involuntary integration of peripheral populations into the global capitalist order requires the intensified participation of metropolitan citizens. As a result, a significant sector of the national population develops a corporate interest in the maintenance of coercive international economic structures. Indeed, given the imperial state's pivotal role in the economy, even a failure to control anti-imperialist challenges can strengthen the public's support for imperialism. A popular revulsion against the "enemies of the state," a search for a resurgence of "lost" national honor and pride become all too common characteristics of an imperialist nation on the defensive.

This popular identification with the state can, however, be traced to more than the immediate interests that significant sectors of the population have in the maintenance of imperial ties. Beyond this particularity lies a generalized support for national economic power and security. The internationalization of capitalist competition does not weaken this tendency. Rather, the expanded scope of accumulation places added pressures on the state to guarantee the national population's accustomed standard of life. In this context, any disruption of the normal international order—even if this order has secularly weakened the nation-state's ability to construct and maintain the national economy—can increase general support for imperialist politics. And this is buttressed by the legitimating ideologies of national power and prestige that have evolved in response to past international tensions.[60]

Beyond these two relatively narrow economic reasons, the strengthening of statist/imperialist ideologies may also rest on other fundamental materialist bases. Marxist-Feminist theorists have long noted that the exercise of male privilege is at the root of all military institutions and that the definitions of maleness and thus the social order of most complex societies depend on the maintenance of a

---

[60] There is an important exception to this process. We would not expect small metropolitan states with few military resources to experience the same sort of imperialist mobilization. Different historically-conditioned possibilities for state action do shape popular ideology.

strong state.[61] If this is true, then any challenge from the periphery threatens more than political-economic stability. Other fundamental institutions of social reproduction—particularly the family—also fall under implicit attack. This admittedly speculative hypothesis may help explain why militarist and familialist ideologies often seem so closely intertwined. It may be that, like the Tsarist state in pre-revolutionary Russia, the state and those leaders that personify the state are still our "little fathers."

A similar argument can be made with respect to race. Certainly, the Western imperialist past has relied on virulent ideologies of racial and national supremacy. The exact character of this chauvinism has varied with the domestic and international historical environment, but few could deny the extent to which racial and/or national bigotry have solidified the concept of "the national interest" and thereby justified the continued maintenance of enormous material divisions between the world's peoples.

Conclusion

Throughout the post-war era, radical political economists have attempted to analyze those political-economic processes in the periphery that help reproduce subservient Third World social formations. Within this general framework, debates have raged fiercely: Has metropolitan capital simply imposed its will on dependent, but resistant national populations? If not, what is the nature of the collaboration and conflict within the "quadruple alliance" of advanced capital, the imperialist state(s), peripheral capital and "its" governmental structures? The studies spawned by these controversies have yielded important new conceptualizations of the nature of imperialist subordination, but they cannot by themselves unravel the most basic theoretical question: Why is it appropriate to assume an internationally coercive metropolitan impulse?

Imperialism and capitalism are intimately related, but not because there is a necessity for the super-exploitation of external territories. Rather, the real benefits that individual corporations and

---

[61] This does not mean that women are morally superior or inherently more peaceful than men. Rather, women and men's participation in imperialist institutions is strongly conditioned by oppressive gender relations. See Enloe and di Leonardo [56] and [50] on this subject.

institutions receive from capital expansion are transmitted politically and culturally to the population as a whole. State agents, often utilizing racially and sexually charged rhetoric, are able to induce large sectors of the population to support the politics of oppression. The success of the advocates of imperialism is not due to especially clever manipulations. The expansion of capital, by permitting the integration of large sectors of the populace into metropolitan-sponsored foreign activities, makes large sectors of the population susceptible to this politics. Moreover, during non-revolutionary times, there is a clear general interest in national economic security, and such a mass desire can lead to popular support for efforts by center powers to "stabilize" the global environment.

Despite this compelling historical logic, the reproduction of imperialism is a problematic process. The ideology of control can be challenged on the basis of other strands within incoherent national cultures. Furthermore, the material interest in foreign activities is not uniform and, indeed, during certain periods of history, one can argue that the prosperity of most citizens is actually harmed by foreign entanglements. The forces producing capitalist imperialism are certainly strong and deeply rooted, but the possibility of the economic and political collapse of imperialist structures is nevertheless real.

D. The Future of Imperialism

International crisis and the Marxian tradition
At the root of imperial oppression lies the permanent anticipation of social crisis. Moreover, this fear has a powerful rational core: from the perspective of the pervasive imperialist interests that form within the metropolitan social formation, "things" threaten to "fall apart" in the periphery far too often.

A chronic expectation of crisis, however, should not imply that the world is always *in* crisis. If this word is to have a sharp meaning, it should refer to particular historical conjunctures—periods in which a specific social order is called into question by political struggle. As Andre Gunder Frank suggests in [69, p. 109], this perspective implies that crisis is a time of transformation as well as conflict.

The crisis is a period in which a diseased social, economic, and political body or system cannot live on as before and is obliged, on pain of death, to undergo transformation that will give it a new lease on life.

Even within this more focussed approach some ambiguities remain. It is still necessary to form qualitative, historically-informed judgements about the nature of social conflict and the possibilities of transformation. Moreover, *crisis* is often used to refer to a sectoral difficulty, which may or may not threaten the entire social order. A financial crisis—in which, as a result of institutional failure, there is intense struggle to change the workings of the banking system—may lead to significant reform without the whole framework of society being either called into question or fundamentally changed.[62]

The general Marxian approach to crisis recognizes the possibility that serious sectoral difficulties can remain isolated and contained. On the other hand, interruptions in the normal functioning of political economic mechanisms are always potentially disruptive of the entire social fabric; the prolongation of economic instability erodes those political and ideological practices that sustain the material order. As with the specific explanation of imperial oppression, however, an explanation of generalized crisis requires the specification of those processes which connect the contradictions of accumulation to social consolidation or disintegration.

Theorists, not surprisingly, disagree on the relative weight which should be given to economic and political processes. Makoto Itoh, for example, stresses the importance of analyzing the contradictions of accumulation abstractly; that is, separately from the political divisions of the world economy. He suggests in [95] that the fundamental starting-point for Marxian theory is the recognition that crisis is both a response to and a mechanism for overcoming the overproduction of capital in relation to the laboring population. In a different way, Wallerstein also stresses in [186] the importance of an

---

[62] The perspective on sectoral crisis—as distinct from general crisis—permits a more subtle interpretation of certain periods of social breakdown. The Great Depression in the United States, for instance, could be better interpreted as an era in which a series of quite sharp sectoral crises were partially contained by Roosevelt's New Deal. At no point, however, could it be reasonably maintained that the whole framework of the social order was in jeopardy. This could be contrasted with the general political crisis in Germany immediately after World War I.

underlying economic focus. The hypothesized divisions among the core, semi-periphery and periphery can only shift during particular "moments" of crisis—moments that are stimulated by downturns in the Kondratiev cycle.

An alternative method is to posit that any given period of capital expansion is governed by a particular political structure of the world economy. During the beginning phase of expansion, certain mechanisms of regulation effectively guarantee the expanded reproduction of capital. This stability, however, is presumed to rest on certain relations of power that are eventually eroded by the uneven development dynamic basic to global accumulation.[63]

Despite the sometimes eclectic nature of regulation theories, this approach is superior to those which place major emphasis on deriving the economic mechanisms of crisis. This is true for two reasons: no narrow economic explanations of economic rupture have succeeded in establishing a compelling empirical or theoretical account of capitalist crisis; and second, all Marxian descriptions of prolonged economic and social disruption must eventually focus on those political and ideological processes that stimulate regulatory breakdown and its reconstruction.

The first point—that crisis theory has failed in deriving economic mechanisms of breakdown—is controversial and deserves more extensive consideration than I can offer here. Nevertheless, the general argument is straightforward: either the theoretical claims for the economic theories of breakdown are logically flawed, or it has not been effectively demonstrated that the key economic contradictions highlighted by these theories must culminate in a political-economic rupture. The excess commodities theories of underconsumption or disproportionality, for instance, can in principle be overcome by Keynesian policy. Taken by themselves, these perspectives cannot explain why the state might not intervene. If, as Baran and Sweezy maintained in [18], capitalist social relations prevent the state from rationally readjusting demand, then we are no longer considering a theory of crisis which derives breakdown from the "pure" logic of capital.

---

[63] This perspective can and has been related to Kondratiev or long-wave analyses. See [186] for an example of this synthesis. For our purposes, however, it is best to keep these "political" and "economic" approaches conceptually separate.

The excess capital theories also suffer from theoretical and empirical ambiguities. On the one hand, there is no logical reason to suppose that the general rate of profit must fall as a result of a rising organic composition of capital—quite the contrary.[64] Furthermore, those who instead derive a cyclical pattern or imminent tendency from Marx's law of the tendency of the rate of profit to fall fail to explain why the state cannot devalorize backward capital through the promotion of a planned expansion. As with the excess commodity perspective, a full explanation of economic rupture requires a theory of state action and reaction. Finally, the alternative excess capital theories of Itoh in [95] and, to some extent, Arrighi in [15]—that capital expands beyond the supplies of labor and raw materials—also lack empirical and theoretical persuasiveness. It is not clear why, with the internationalization of capital, shortfalls in raw material production could not be overcome.[65] The thesis of labor shortage is more compelling because capital does not directly regulate the production of labor power. Nevertheless, it has not been convincingly demonstrated that this "shortage" has been a prime cause of economic stagnation—especially since the expansion of capital has bred (with the exception of Japan) an enormous flow of labor from the near-periphery to the advanced capitalist world.

This theoretical disarray is a matter of serious concern. On the other hand, few Marxist (and non-Marxist) explanations of specific crisis periods have ever solely focussed on economic variables. The central theme of nearly all analyses of the Great Depression, for example, is that the 1930s troubles were partially caused and then prolonged by international political disorganization. As Kindleberger notes in [105], the unwillingness of the US to provide long-term credit to the exhausted European World War I combatants was a major source of the economic collapse, and this failure in turn stemmed from the inability of the most powerful nation-states to control inter-imperialist rivalries.

---

[64] See John Roemer's analysis in [156, pp. 87–133].

[65] For a brief discussion of raw material supply constraints and capital accumulation, see Albert Szymanski's analysis in [171, pp. 152–168]. This does not imply that the competition for raw materials is an unimportant aspect of international competition. Michael Tanzer provides impressive documentation of this process in [173]. Rather, the claim is that this problem cannot comprise a general explanation of imperialism.

This pragmatic appeal to past scholarly findings does have a theoretical basis. While the disruption of an international order is rooted in intensified capitalist competition and uneven development, global disintegration cannot simply be explained by referring to erratic rhythms of accumulation. The expanded reproduction of capital does not inevitably generate divisive tendencies; it also can unify previously separate accumulation units. Only a study which unravels the connections among global economic contradictions, nation-state formation and international regulation can hope to determine whether integration or disintegration trends will predominate. A theory of crisis, then, involves a complex analysis of economic and political contradictions. Without this focus, Marxian efforts in this area of study lack all conjunctural specificity and, for this reason, fail to provide useful political guidance.

Orthodox crisis scenarios
It is most useful to begin any discussion of the breakdown of global capitalism by elaborating a series of alternative scenarios—the probability of each depending on the analyst's assessment of the "balance of class forces." Unfortunately these speculative exercises often seem quite arbitrary; the reader is sometimes treated to an ad-hoc analysis in which the possible outcomes of crisis multiply indefinitely and all options appear equally likely. The failure to question the theoretical status of the nation-state especially strengthens this scatter-shot tendency. Instead of grasping what may be fundamentally new in the present order (in this case, the possible decline of the nation-state as an economic regulator) the temptation instead is to employ vague metaphors that refer back loosely to past international difficulties which were dominated by nation-state conflicts.

Nevertheless, the advantages of assessing the plausibility of distinct trajectories of global regulation outweigh these flaws. Without this approach, it would be difficult to assess the possible future directions of global capitalism. Moreover, this approach has the advantage of permitting an escape from a deterministic analysis which considers only one or two cataclysmic results from a breakdown in the mechanisms of imperialist reproduction. A systematic analysis of the future requires a well-articulated understanding of past trends in the evolution of global capitalism.

The challenge to capitalist unity: A breakdown within the advanced capitalist west?
In the early twentieth century, most theorists of imperialism assumed that the periphery would be oppressed whether or not the advanced capitalist countries were unified. Indeed, the general argument was that intensified rivalry would stimulate more oppressive forms of colonial rule over sectors of the Third World. Thus, Kautsky was able to represent his model of ultra-imperialism as a preferable, more benign framework for capitalist development.[66] Today, the tables have been turned. It is generally agreed that some form of advanced capitalist coherence greatly facilitates the North's predominance within the world economy. Without some metropolitan nation-state understandings, it would be possible for the more autonomous Third World states to play off rival imperial claimants against each other and thereby exercise more political-economic power. A break-up of the Western alliance, for example, might lead the European powers to extend a much more liberal package of economic assistance to the Lomé countries in order to maintain some influence in the former colonial territories. Or perhaps Japan would expand its military and economic aid in East Asia in order to buttress its predominant capitalist presence. Unlike the early twentieth century, the competition for influence might so strengthen the position of Third World countries that metropolitan nation-state imperialism might cease altogether.[67]

Despite this shift in the implications of advanced capitalist rivalry, there are certain elements of contemporary economic evolution which do confirm Lenin's central presumptions about the erratic nature of capitalist growth. In particular, neo-Leninists often maintain that the process of uneven development must eventually erode the US state's ability to maintain itself as the hegemonic capitalist power. At this point, presumably during a crisis period, one could expect an outbreak of prolonged intrametropolitan conflict, as the more robust capitalist economies compete for their place in the political sun.

---

[66] See Salvadori's analysis in [160, pp. 322–3] for the full statement of Kautsky's unity perspective.
[67] Kidron in [103] was one of the first post-war Marxist analysts to address this possibility.

The data supporting the thesis of US economic decline are, at first glance, compelling. Earlier sections have documented the decline in the US share in global economic activity. But even if this particular manifestation of the uneven development thesis is granted, two further questions still have to be answered before the capitalist rivalry thesis can be accepted:

1) Does a decline in economic competitiveness really indicate a decline in US political economic hegemony?

2) Even if it does become impossible for the United States to maintain its global influence, does this "fall from grace" necessarily imply a breakdown in advanced capitalist cohesion?

The first question arises because US predominance in the advanced capitalist world has rested on much more than American economic supremacy. The construction of military alliances and other agreements of "defense" cooperation have been just as important for the maintenance of the US empire, and there are short-term and long-term reasons why such understandings might continue even as economic relations of power shift. The emergence of autonomous peripheral Third World capitalist states and the construction of a hostile non-capitalist bloc of nations under the domination of the Soviet Union provide a strong impulse for military cooperation. In this geopolitical context, the United States is very well placed to exert its influence. And to the extent that issues of economic and military coordination fuse, subordinate allies will be under strong pressure to promote commercial cooperation as well.

On the economic level, the deepening of the internationalization of capital has also given further impetus to advanced capitalist unity. Recent developments make it possible to imagine a system of economic regulation that no longer rests on the actions of a single nation-state, but rather, on a series of negotiations coordinated through new international negotiating fora. The International Monetary Fund, for instance, has played a key role in disciplining both certain advanced capitalist and Third World economies, and the OECD has also increasingly served as an important site for sectoral economic discussions. Even United States policy has been subject to some global restraints. The dramatic turn-around in monetary policy in the late 1970s and early 1980s has been widely interpreted as a partial response to intensifying European pressures to halt the devaluation of the dollar.[68]

This last argument will seem counter-intuitive to some. Many European Marxist theorists have suggested that the collapse of fixed exchange rates during the early 1970s signalled the beginning of a period of economic chaos that cannot be resolved until a new hegemonic power is able to restore discipline within a new Bretton Woods.[69] It is undoubtedly true that the economic world is more subject to erratic movements than it was during the 1950s and 1960s. In addition, shifts in competitive relations have led to a sharp increase in the governmental management of international trade. Some analysts, for example, have estimated that as much as thirty-five percent of US manufactured imports are now subject to non-tariff controls.[70] Fewer theorists have noted, however, that these orderly marketing agreements and unilateral import quota arrangements have been consistently linked to the further *integration* of the world economy. In almost every case, such measures have encouraged the international movements of productive capital either into the protected country directly, or towards countries whose exports are not being restricted. And even in those cases where foreign investment patterns have not been significantly affected, workers in the protected industries have had to adjust their work practices and wage benefits in order to respond to the devalorizing threat from the outside world.[71]

This pattern reflects an underlying continuity in the world economy. Since the late 1940s, finance and productive capital movements have become progressively less subject to direct governmental regulation. The advent of floating exchange rates has reduced even further the likelihood that any individual capitalist

---

[68] During the late 1970s and early 1980s, international financial concern about the future of the dollar intensified markedly. European business and political leaders increasingly placed pressure on the United States to reform its policies, although this advice was not particularly coherent.

[69] Ricardo Parboni in [145] is best known for this position, and Block provides in [25] an historical accounting of the rise and fall of Bretton Woods from a similar perspective.

[70] Lawrence in [108, pp. 120–1] cites this figure and refers to an article by Bela and Carol Belassa, "Industrial Protection in the Developed Countries."

[71] For a general overview of these relations, see Andreef's analysis in [12].

70   J. WILLOUGHBY

state will impose unilateral trade and capital controls. This does not mean that the nation-state is now powerless; monetary and fiscal policy can be used to engage in "dirty floating" and subidies can be granted in order to attract capital flows or increase the competitiveness of exports. These actions do increase nation-state antagonisms. Nevertheless, these contradictions take place within the context of progressive capital internationalization. Today, the struggles among the advanced capitalist states are about the nature of the insertion of each national economy into this process. As a result, private capital movements, backed by occasional interventions by the IMF, have become increasingly important in determining the nature of exchange and production relations within the advanced capitalist economies. This is not because national capital has lost power in some unspecified sense, but rather results from the stability of those basic political understandings that have permitted the increasing multilateralization of all sectors of capital throughout the metropolitan world.[72]

The new dynamics of capital expansion and the "a-national" regulatory institutions that have emerged with this internationalization process raise a major challenge to the post-Leninist model of international collapse. Unlike the pre-war and inter-war periods of the early twentieth century, the assessment of any national economy's strength requires the drawing of a sharp distinction between the material circumstances of the general population and the position of capital owned by national citizens. The declining competitiveness of the U.S. economy, for example, has not inhibited the most important sectors of U.S. capital from adapting themselves to new economic conditions. As long as the social pain of capital restructuring does not produce new forms of anti-capitalist struggle, the domestic base for US capital internationalization can remain strong. This is one more reason why we should not mechanistically expect a breakdown in advanced capitalist coherence.

The collapse of metropolitan domination: The revolt of the Third World?
The political autonomy of the Third World has clearly restrained

---

[72] Radice makes a similar argument in [151].

the options of metropolitan capitalist states. Western attempts to resolve internal tensions of uneven development can no longer replicate earlier colonialist struggles for territory, and this is one of the major factors making a significant intensification of metropolitan rivalry unlikely. Paradoxically, this weakening in the power of individual nation-states has strengthened the position of metropolitan capital as a whole. Capital penetration and the corresponding consolidation of capitalist social relations has rarely slackened in the post-war period.[73]

Nevertheless, it is possible to argue that this strong position rests on unstable political and economic foundations. The drive for Third World political autonomy must eventually challenge capitalist prerogatives, and the contradictions of capitalist growth in the periphery will permit an anti-imperialist revolutionary breakthrough that cannot be contained by the advanced capitalist world. This perspective, which can draw on both Maoist and Trotskyist traditions, is a Third Worldist mirror image of Luxemburg's thesis of capitalist crisis: instead of capital expansion shrinking the non-capitalist areas of production available for exploitation, the capitalist sectors of the Third World will transform themselves through political struggle into non-capitalist entities.

During the heady days of Chinese cultural revolution, little thought was given to the alternative. A nationally-based anti-imperialist revolt might actually strengthen certain contemporary structures of metropolitan domination. In particular, new military ties and new forms of financial and productive capital investment could serve to re-link more politically autonomous national social formations to the logic of capital internationalization. Both the Maoist encirclement and Trotskyist permanent revolution analyses correctly pinpoint the sources of peripheral revolt without noting that the same instabilities may drive triumphant nationalist leaders to form "more favorable" alliances with the imperial center.

The experience of Vietnam provides a good example of this process. During and after the "fall" of Indochina in the early 1970s, many predicted that the whole region of South East Asia would become progressively hostile to metropolitan capital. An examination of US imperial reaction to this setback, however, reveals a

---

[73] O'Connor [140] and Nabudere [138] strongly make this point.

quite different process. After some indecision, new alliances with
the Peoples Republic of China and the continuation of close links
with the states surrounding Indochina effectively isolated this
region—thereby intensifying the starvation of war-devastated
masses and forcing Vietnam into an even closer embrace with the
Soviet Union. By most accounts, this region today desperately
requires infusions of capital and technological assistance for its
development projects. If there is to be any shift in geopolitical
relations, it is more likely that we will witness a gradual rapproche-
ment with the West, rather than an expanding zone of state-socialist
economies in South East Asia.[74]

If national, anti-capitalist revolt by itself is not likely to disinte-
grate the global capitalist order, it is still possible that the global
economy will eventually suffer from a series of irredeemable
breakdowns. If this occurred, it could be plausible to hypothesize
that local rebellions would spark significant regional unravellings of
the capitalist order. Certainly, the oil price shocks of the 1970s and
the debt crises of the early 1980s can be interpreted as signalling
eventual political-economic collapse. On the other hand, the
sectoral crises of the recent past also carry with them a far different
implication—one which highlights the unifying and differentiating
power of global capitalism.

The OPEC crisis, for instance, reveals the close, interdependent
ties that existed between Middle Eastern governments and the
global oil companies. The increased autonomy of these Third World
states allowed the elites of these regions to command a portion of
the enormous oil rents that would have been unheard of twenty
years before. This success, however, depended on the continuing
operation of the marketing and distribution networks of the global
oil companies. Thus, during a period of increased demand, a
devaluing dollar and rising production costs in the United States, it
was possible for both metropolitan oil capital and the OPEC states
to share in the bounty. This is hardly a story of Third World revolt.
It is true that the oil shock did severely disrupt the metropolitan
domestic economies, but it does not follow that such harm (in the

---

[74] Chomsky and Herman describe U.S. resurgence in South East Asia in [39],
while White analyzes Vietnam's recent development experience in [190].

form of inflation and unemployment) represents more than the sharp and erratic adjustment of exchange and production relations between two, increasingly integrated sectors of the world economy.[75]

The shifts in capital flows that resulted from the events of the 1970s are closely connected to the debt crises of the 1980s. Metropolitan banks became able to tap the enormously increased liquidity of the OPEC states and "recycle" these funds to the "Newly Industrializing Countries" (NICs) of South America and East Asia. As the earlier section on the internationalization of capital documents, the Third World today can be classified into at least two distinct categories: those "richer" nations that are primarily dependent on private funds for international liquidity, and those poorer nations which receive the bulk of their foreign finance from the bilateral and multilateral "aid-giving" institutions. Even with the striking fall of OPEC surpluses and the drying up of new bank lending to many of the NICs, this bifurcated pattern has continued. It is unlikely that the countries which became primarily dependent on private credit during the previous decade can ever return to public funds for infusions of additional capital.

The debt burden for Latin American NICs is now intense and the living standards of the bulk of the population in many countries have fallen sharply during the early 1980s. Nevertheless, there is little indication that a unified resistance to metropolitan bank usury is developing. Instead, each nation is taking advantage (or suffering from) its unique status in the global economy. The numerous ad-hoc negotiations coordinated by the IMF and the distinct character of each debt rescheduling agreement reveal this process sharply.[76] The need to import necessary agricultural and industrial products can make even the most nationalistic and anti-imperialist state planner reluctant to break credit links. It is never clear when it would be propitious to take such a drastic step. Despite the present harsh austerity and the strong possibility that it will continue well

---

[75] Tanzer and Zorn suggest this assessment of OPEC in [174].

[76] The 1984 Argentine case is especially instructive. Its efforts to encourage the coordination of global bargaining were essentially undercut by the separate rescheduling agreements of Brazil and Mexico.

into the next decade,[77] any break with metropolitan capital would, in the short-term, impoverish the renegade national economy even further.

There is a dynamic similarity between these general North-South developments and the role which the evolving world economy has played in determining political economic relations within the metropolitan core. Economic difficulties have become associated with the emergence of surprisingly stable *ad-hoc* international capitalist regulatory mechanisms.

It is always possible that continued stagnation will eventually rupture the contemporary practices of the "quadruple alliance." The fragile resurrections of Argentinian and Brazilian parliamentary democracy in the context of severe economic crisis, for instance, could be read as promising this development. This potential, however, should not blind us to contemporary reality. Nation-state relations between North and South have been strained as a result of the early 1980s economic collapse, but, so far, the crisis of material production has not challenged the global capitalist order.

Instead, flows of private capital have increasingly come to determine Third World economic evolution. This development does not eliminate nation-state conflict, nor even the sometimes effective manipulation of some market variables through state policy. But the discourse of North-South nation-state conflict has shifted: since the early 1970s, the New International Economic Order rhetoric of the Group of 77 has focussed on reorganizing market structures by limiting the power of transnational corporations and guaranteeing Third World export earnings. In short, the struggle has been waged over the nature of Third World integration into global capitalism— not the question of integration itself. As in the metropolitan world, the absence of far-reaching shifts in the framework of domestic and

---

[77] The 1980–5 period has been disastrous for most African nations (a 1/6% *per annum* decrease in *per capita* GDP). The "middle income" developing nations also experienced a sustained decrease in *per capita* GDP during this period. The World Bank estimates in [194, pp. 34–6] that if industrial country performance does not improve over the next decade then African *per capita* income will continue to shrink (although at a lower rate) and most other developing nations' growth will be consistently lower than that experienced during the 1970s. Even the optimistic William R. Cline has labelled the 1980s as the lost decade for Latin America. For Cline's analysis, see [40].

international political struggle has so far foreclosed other anti-capitalist options.

A new crisis scenario: The generalization of imperialism and the logic of exterminism
The two orthodox theories of imperial breakdown are not compelling because neither considers the shifting implications of nationality in the contemporary world. The imperial rivalry school fails to note that it is increasingly difficult to identify consolidated and opposed national capitalist interests in each metropolitan social formation. On the other hand, the Third World revolt scenario normally discounts the crucial and divisive role that the nation-state plays in the formation of capitalism in the periphery. Correcting these gaps forces one to conclude that the internationalization of capital continues to rest on strong political-economic foundations.

There are, nevertheless, some unspoken assumptions in this analysis that should be clarified. It has, for instance, been taken for granted that popular opposition to imperialism's workings is unlikely to develop within advanced capitalist societies. There are good reasons for this premise—not the least of which is the formation of powerful, but routinized, imperial cultures in most metropolitan social formations. On the other hand, there have always been signs (especially in Europe and Japan) that popular acceptance of the structures of global politics is unstable. No sweeping assumptions about the future nature of oppositional politics are ever that secure.

A second implicit assumption of the preceding analysis is that the dynamics of imperial oppression—if not challenged effectively by new social movements—can always produce a stable social order. In other words, without a qualitative shift in class politics, imperialism cannot self-destruct. This is a classic Marxian assumption, since it is generally argued that significant social changes can only take place through the conscious or unconscious manifestations of class politics. True, radical theorists from Marx onwards have expressed the premonition that capitalism will collapse under the accumulated weight of intensifying contradictions, even without the direct intervention of the working class. Nevertheless, few Marxian theorists have speculated about the possible mechanisms of disintegration into chaos. The slogan "Socialism or Barbarism" remains a grand theatrical appeal that evokes the prophets of the Old Testament rather than provoking scientific inquiry.

It is no longer necessary to remain on this rhetorical level. The reproduction of metropolitan domination is associated with the spread of capitalist social relations, the emergence of quasi-autonomous Third World states, the intensification of nationalist conflict within the South, and the consequent progressive militarization of global politics. Although a strange sort of peace has reigned within the center, the last two decades in particular have been associated with an intensified arms trade and the regular waging of catastrophic warfare in the periphery.[78] It is, therefore, reasonable to ask whether or not the present structure and practices of global politics can continue. And, given the enormous advances in the technology of warfare, it is now possible to specify the meaning of barbarism more precisely. At stake is the actual elimination of a large portion, if not all, of humanity.

For the purposes of this essay, there are two aspects to the exterminism scenario: the generalization of imperial conflict throughout the Third World and the particular modalities of conflict between the US and the Soviet Union.[79] In both cases, the mechanisms of domination that are inextricably linked to the expansion of metropolitan capital have laid the basis for the consolidation of autonomous imperialist practices within peripheral states.

It is easier to develop this argument with respect to the capitalist Third World than the Soviet Union—where the intensity of cold-war rhetoric often obscures the tight interdependence between metropolitan and Soviet imperialisms. I have already argued that capital internationalization is closely connected to the articulation of new nationalist ideologies and the importation of new and sophisticated mechanisms of military coercion. This combination has often resulted in powerful, expansionist tendencies, and as neighboring

---

[78] For documentation of the rising arms trade to the Third World, growing internal arms production in this region and the chronic waging of warfare, see Ruth Leger Sivard, statistical presentations in [165].

[79] A further exterminist angle that will not be considered here is that articulated by Green Party theorist Rudolf Bahro [16], who foresees the ecological collapse of the globe. The theory of exterminism on which we will focus is largely taken from E. P. Thompson's articles [176] and [177].

Third World states are experiencing the same process, the possibility of fractricidal conflict is great. There is a material basis to this powerful evocation of national integrity: nation-state consolidation takes place in an atmosphere of crisis; distinct social groupings are articulating and struggling for alternative visions of national homogeneity. From these contradictions arise pressures to quell internal "enemies of the state" and meet the challenges posed by external Third World and metropolitan nations. It is not surprising that this process often culminates in the intensified presence and use of military institutions within the peripheral state.

The metropolitan powers have participated in this process; often, their specific actions have sparked intense divisions within the Third World and encouraged the militarization of entire regions. Nevertheless, the periphery is not always manipulated by the North in a straightforward way. This is especially evident in the aftermath of specific social/political revolutions. The case of the 1980s Iran/Iraq war is the most dramatic recent example of metropolitan inability to contain political and military conflict. Although new tentacles of political-economic control are reorganized by the imperial powers, there is always the possibility that this exercise of imperialist politics will fail. This potential for breakdown beomes more pronounced as Third World states acquire the ability to manufacture sophisticated military equipment for themselves. The generalization of imperialist politics leads the metropolitan social formations into an ever more dangerous round of global politics that can eventually threaten the security of the citizens of the metropolitan world.[80]

As a starting point, this analysis of the derivative imperialisms of Third World states can be applied to the Soviet Union. Trotsky himself pointed out that the extreme backwardness of inherited economic and social conditions combined with external imperial pressure to stimulate a renewal of an authoritarian Russian nationalism that centered on the imprecise slogan: "Socialism within One Country."[81] It is also necessary to add the centrifugal threat of

---

[80] Nowhere is this process clearer than in the Middle East. The US is an active participant in and thus responsible for an evolving politics that seems increasingly uncontrollable and life-threatening. See the analysis of Noam Chomsky in [38].
[81] For an analysis of Trotsky's perspective, see [48, pp. 34–5].

non-Russian nationalist politics after 1917. This led to an eventual
Bolshevik breaking of Lenin's promise to grant self-determination
to all minority nationalities within the borders of the old empire.
Finally, the internationalist commitment to export the revolution
was transformed at a quite early stage into a justification for
practices of external and internal coercion. The explicitly imperial
Brezhnev doctrine of "proletarian internationalism" has its origins
in the aborted Red Army invasion of Poland in 1920.[82]

The radical reorganization of social life in the Soviet Union
combined with this new expression of imperial state power led to a
predictable metropolitan response; after World War I joint policies
were introduced to isolate the "socialist cancer" through the
construction of new alliances with anti-Soviet regimes immediately
around its borders. Until World War II, Soviet-Western relations
can be interpreted within the framework already developed for
metropolitan-peripheral relations during the post-war period. And
if this global conflict had not occurred, the concerted pressures on
this non-capitalist territory might have eventually culminated in a
clearer subordination of the USSR to capitalist imperialism.

Mid-twentieth century history, however, turned out quite
differently. Despite the staggering devastation of the war in the
USSR, Stalin was able to redraw the map of Eastern Europe to give
the Soviet Union a much larger field of autonomy. In addition, the
technological independence of the USSR allowed it to compete with
the United States on a military level—at first symbolically and then
practically. These two breakthroughs signalled a qualitative shift for
the nature of capitalist imperialism. In the periphery, a bi-polar
world of global tension became the political framework under which

---

[82] Charles Bellelheim describes in [23, pp. 419–28] Lenin's deathbed concern about
Stalin's development of policies that would subordinate non-Russian nationalities.
But Lenin was not blameless in this matter. Deutscher in his account of the 1920
invasion of Poland notes that Lenin was an enthusiastic proponent of this action
(against the isolated Trotsky). While the decision could be justified as a legitimate
response to the Polish invasion of the Ukraine, Lenin did eventually admit his error
in attempting to export revolution by arms. As Deutscher notes in [47, p. 471]:
The error was neither fortuitous nor inconsequential. It had its origin in the
Bolshevik horror of isolation in the world, a horror shared by all leaders of the party
but affecting their actions differently . . . The march on Warsaw had been a desperate
attempt to break out of that isolation. The idea of revolution by conquest had been
injected into the Bolshevik mind; and it went on to ferment and fester.

the accelerated expansion of both capitalist social relations and anti-imperialist revolts in the Third World took place. In Europe, the newly-found capitalist unity of the West was purchased at the expense of a rigidly divided Europe—a freezing of autonomous socialist and nationalist politics in this region. As Thompson notes in [176], this is the real social meaning of the Cold War.

This unstable framework of co-existence is associated with the unprecedented stockpiling of weapons of extermination. The detente so hailed during the 1970s quickly collapsed—as both the United States and the Soviet Union were forced and encouraged to respond to new eruptions of Third World unrest and new technological breakthroughs in nuclear arms competition. Thus, Third World contradictions have interacted with U.S.–Soviet conflict to expand all aspects of the arms race. Given the complex interconnections of regional and global imperial tensions, and the sophistication, sensitivity and power of all new weapons systems, it is not difficult to imagine how a technological or political miscalculation could culminate in a generalized global conflict beyond the control of any nation-state leadership.

In short, the exterminist thesis of imperial breakdown rests on strong theoretical and empirical foundations. The religious intimations of a collapsing world now have a scientific basis. The ever expanding "advances" in the forces of destruction can only be temporarily and imperfectly controlled by contemporary political institutions; society's continued existence requires a transformation in the social organization of economic and political life. The revolutionary implications of this analysis present all of humanity with unprecedentedly cruel choices. Either we work to interrupt and reverse the dynamics of imperial conflict in the hope that such a politics is not in itself destabilizing, or we watch the exterminist logic of today's international conflicts unfold while praying that the universally recognized danger of nuclear war somehow imposes constraints and rationality on the global political order.

3. CONCLUSION

In this essay, I have taken issue with many of the fundamentals of the classic Leninist theory of imperialism. Imperialism does not represent a special stage in the development of capitalism; uneven

development does not always culminate in the breakdown of
capitalist order; there is no necessity for the super-exploitation of
the periphery by metropolitan capital; and, consequently, it is
possible for some Third World economies to develop sophisticated
industrial capitalist structures.

Rejecting the familiar nostrums of the dominant Marxist theory is
essential if a materialist framework is to address the evolving
dynamics of capitalist imperialism. Leninist theorists have been able
to explain a set of cyclical processes—war and economic division
and degeneration being the major ones—with some superficial
plausibility. On the other hand, the standard analyses of qualitative
change, of those macroscopic anomalies that Arrighi referred to in
this essay's opening passage, have been much less successful. The
declining significance of inter-metropolitan capitalist war, the rise of
"a-national" capitalist regulatory mechanisms, the growing power
of expansionist impulses in certain key Third World and non-
capitalist states—and the increasing possibility that these processes
will bring about the end of human life itself—all of these shifts in
the imperialist experience can be better explained by an alternative
Marxist framework.

This alternative recognizes that:

1) Capital expansion has always been a powerful force behind the
global differentiation of the world economy.

2) This economic differentiation is simultaneously linked to the
rise of imperialist and subordinated national social formations
within the capitalist world economy.

3) The resulting polarities of the world economy are not frozen,
but continually evolving as a result of shifts in class structures and
technological capabilities. In particular, the populations in each
Third World capitalist social formation must contend with the
constantly changing contours of a quadruple alliance among metropolitan capitals, metropolitan states, local peripheral capitals and
the Third World state.

4) These disruptions have tended to strengthen imperialist politics and culture in the major states of the capitalist world, even
while threatening the ongoing frameworks of capitalist political-
economic management.

5) Imperialism is not a feature of capitalist nation-state behavior that is unique to the metropolitan world. Nevertheless, the imperialistic impulses that exist in non-capitalist and peripheral nation-states have been largely structured by the histories of metropolitan capital and nation-state expansion.

This alternative sustains one key finding of the Leninist theory: that capitalism and imperialism are inextricably linked. On the other hand, it rejects the stage-theoretic framework and its attendant attempt to describe the static characteristics of capitalism in each hypothesized historical epoch. If there is one aspect of capitalist imperialism that all analysts should recognize, it is its heterogeneous character—both in history and in the contemporary world. The concepts exist within the Marxist framework to embrace this variety. Indeed, no other economic theory can as effectively describe and explain shifts in the capital accumulation process, and no political theory has as persuasively linked these economic tendencies to the formation of contemporary political and ideological practices. The detour of the Leninist tradition notwithstanding, this rich analytic heritage provides a key foundation for any analysis of contemporary international oppression and conflict.

References

[1] Abdel-Malik, A., *Nation and Revolution*. Albany, N.Y.: State University of New York Press, 1982.
[2] Adelman, I., and C. T. Morris, *Economic Growth and Social Equity in Developing Countries*. Stanford: Stanford University Press, 1973.
*[3] Aglietta, M., "World Capitalism in the Eighties," *New Left Review* **136** (November-December 1982).
[4] Alavi, H., and T. Shanin (Eds), *Introduction to the Sociology of Developing Countries*. New York: Monthly Review Press, 1982.
[5] Alexander, R. J., *The Tragedy of Chile*. Westport, Conn.: Greenwood Press, 1978.
**[6] Amin, S., *Class and Nation: Historically and in the Current Crisis*. New York: Monthly Review Press 1980.
[7] Amin, S., "The Class Structure of the Contemporary Imperialist System," *Monthly Review* **31** (January 1980).
[8] Amin, S., *The Law of Value and Historical Materialism*. New York: Monthly Review Press, 1978.
[9] Amin, S., *Unequal Development*. New York: Monthly Review Press, 1976.
*[10] Anderson, B., *Imagined Communities: Reflections on the Origins and Spread of Nationalism*. London: Verso, 1983.
[11] Anderson, P., *Lineages of the Absolutist State*. London: Verso, 1979.

*[12] Andreef, W., "The International Centralization of Capital and the Re-
      ordering of World Capitalism," *Capital and Class* **22** (Spring 1984), 59–80.
*[13] Andreef, W., *Les Multinationales hors la Crise*. Paris: Le Sycomore, 1982.
*[14] Arrighi, G., "A Crisis of Hegemony," in *Dynamics of Global Crisis*. New
      York: Monthly Review Press, 1982.
*[15] Arrighi, G., *The Geometry of Imperialism*. London: NLB, 1978.
**[16] Bahro, R., *Socialism and Survival*. London: Heretic Books, 1982.
 [17] Baran, P., *The Political Economy of Growth*.
**[18] Baran, P., and P. Sweezy, *Monopoly Capital*. New York: Monthly Review
      Press, 1966.
 [19] Barnet, R., and R. E. Muller, *Global Reach: The Power of the Multinational
      Corporation*. New York: Simon and Schuster, 1974.
*[20] Barnett, A., "Iron Britannica," *New Left Review* **134** (July–August 1982).
**[21] Barone, C. A., "Dependency, Marxist Theory, and Salvaging the Idea of
      Capitalism in South Korea," *Review of Radical Political Economics* **15**
      (Spring 1983), 43–67.
 [22] Barratt Brown, M., *Essays on Imperialism*. Nottingham, Eng.: Spokesman
      Books, 1972.
**[23] Bettelheim, C., *Class Struggle in the USSR: First Period*: 1917–23, trans. by
      Brian Pearce. New York: Monthly Review Press, 1976.
 [24] Bleaney, M. F., *Underconsumption Theories: A History and Critical
      Analysis*. New York: International Publishers, 1976.
**[25] Block, F., *The Origins of International Economic Disorder*. Berkeley:
      University of California, 1977.
 [26] Bluestone, B. and B. Harrison, *The Deindustrialization of America*. New
      York: Basic Books, 1982.
**[27] Boggs, C., "The Democratic Road: New Departures and Old Problems," in
      The Politics of Eurocommunism, ed. by C. Boggs and D. Plotke. Boston:
      South End Press, 1980, 431–76.
 [28] Brandt Commission: *Common Crisis*. London, Pan Books, 1983.
 [29] Brandt Commission: *North-South: A Program for Survival*. Cambridge,
      Mass., The MIT Press, 1981.
**[30] Braudel, F., *The Structure of Everday Life: Civilisation and Capitalism,
      15th-18th Century*. New York: Harper and Row, 1981.
*[31] Brett, E. A., *International Money and Capitalist Crisis: The Anatomy of
      Global Disintegration*. Boulder, Colo.: Westview Press, 1983.
*[32] Brewer, A., *Marxist Theories of Imperialism: A Critical Survey*. London:
      Routledge and Kegan Paul, 1980.
**[33] Bukharin, N., "Imperialism and the Accumulation of Capital," in
      *Imperialism and the Accumulation of Capital: Rosa Luxemburg and Nikolai
      Bukharin*, ed. by K. J. Tarbuk. London: Allen Lane, Penguin, 1972.
*[34] Bukharin, N., *Imperialism and World Economy*. New York: Monthly
      Review Press, 1973.
 [35] Bunkina, M. K., *USA versus Western Europe: New Trends*. Moscow:
      Progress Publishers, 1979.
 [36] Calleo, D. P., *The Imperious Economy*. Cambridge, Mass.: Harvard Press,
      1982.
 [37] Cardoso, F. H., "Associated-Dependent Development: Theoretical and
      Practical Implications," in *Authoritarian Brazil*, ed. by A. Stepan. New
      Haven: Yale University Press, 1973.
**[38] Chomsky, N., *The Fateful Triangle: The United States, Israel and the
      Palestinians*. Boston: South End Press, 1983.

**[39] Chomsky, N., and E. S. Herman, *After the Cataclysm: Postwar Indochina and the Reconstruction of Imperial Ideology*. Boston: South End Press, 1979.
**[40] Cline, W. R., *International Debt: Systemic Risk and Policy Response*. Washington, D.C.: Institute for International Economics, 1984.
 [41] Cohen, B. J., *The Question of Imperialism: The Political Economy of Dominance and Dependence*. New York: Basic Books, 1973.
**[42] Cottrell, P. J., *British Overseas Investment in the Nineteenth Century*. London: Macmillan Press, 1975.
 [43] Corrigan, P. (ED.), *Capitalism, State Formation and Marxist Theory*. London: Quartet Books, 1980.
 *[44] Cypher, J., "The Internationalization of Capital and the Transition of Social Formations: A Critique of the Monthly Review School," *Review of Radical Political Economics* **11** (Winter 1979), 33–49.
 [45] Cypher, J., "A Prop Not a Burden," *Dollars and Sense* **93** (January 1984).
 *[46] de Janvry, A., and F. Kramer, "The Limits of Unequal Exchange," *Review of Radical Political Economics*" (Winter 1979), 3–15.
**[47] Deutscher, I., *The Prophet Armed: Trotsky: 1879–1921*. London: Oxford University Press, 1954.
 [48] Deutscher, I., *The Prophet Outcast: Trotsky: 1929–40*. New York: Vintage Books, Random House, 1963.
 [49] de Vroey, M., "A Regulation Approach Interpretation of Contemporary Crisis," *Capital and Crisis* **23** (September 1984), 45–66.
[50] di Leonardo, M., "Morals, Mothers and Militarism," *Feminist Studies,* **11 (Fall 1985), 599–618.
 *[51] Dobb, M., "Imperialism," in *Political Economy and Capitalism*. New York: International Publishers, 1945.
**[52] Easterlin, R. A., "American Population since 1900," in *The American Economy in Transition,* ed. by M. Feldstein. Chicago: NBER, University of Chicago Press, 1980.
**[53] Eisenstadt, S. N., *Revolution and the Transformation of Societies: A Comparative Study of Civilizations*. New York: The Free Press, Macmillan, 1978.
 *[54] Emmanuel, A., *Unequal Exchange: A Study of the Imperialism of Trade,* trans. by B. Pearce. New York: Monthly Review Press, 1972.
 [55] Emmanuel, A., "White Settler Colonialism and the Myth of Investment Imperialism," *New Left Review* **73** (May–June, 1972), 35–57.
 *[56] Enloe, C., *Does Khaki Become You? The Militarization of Women's Lives*. London: Pluto Press, 1983.
 *[57] Evans, P., *Dependent Development: The Alliance of Multinational, State and Local Capital in Brazil*. Princeton: Princeton University Press, 1979.
 [58] Evans, P., "Reinventing the Bourgeoisie: State Entrepreneurship and Class Formation in Dependent Capitalist Development," in *Marxist Inquiries: Studies of Labor, Class and States,* ed. by M. Burawoy and T. Skocpol. Chicago: University of Chicago Press, 1982.
**[59] Fanon, F, *The Wretched of the Earth*. New York: Grove Press, 1963.
 [60] Fann, K. T., and D. C. Hodges (Eds.): *Readings in U.S. Imperialism*. Boston: Porter Sargent, 1971.
 [61] Farhang, F., *U.S. Imperialism: From the Spanish American War to the Iranian Revolution*. Boston: South End Press, 1981.
 [62] Feinberg, R. E., *The Intemperate Zone: The Third World Challenge to U.S. Foreign Policy*. New York: Norton, 1983.

84 J. WILLOUGHBY

*[63] Fieldhouse, D., *Economics and Empire: 1830–1914.* Ithaca, N.Y., Cornell University Press, 1973.
[64] Fields, G. S., "Who Benefits from Economic Development? Reply," *American Economic Review* **70 (March 1980), 250–262.
**[65] Fine, B., and L. Harris, *Rereading Capital.* New York: Columbia University Press, 1979.
[66] Fishlow, A., "Who Benefits from Economic Development? Comment," *American Economic Review* **70 (March 1980): 250–262.
**[67] FitzSimons, L., *The Kennedy Doctrine.* New York: Random House, 1972.
[68] Frank, A. G., *Capitalism and Underdevelopment in Latin America: Historical Studies of Chile and Brazil.* New York: Monthly Review Press, 1967.
**[69] Frank, A. G., "Crisis of Ideology and Ideology of Crisis," in *Dynamics of Global Crisis.* New York: Monthly Review Press, 1982.
**[70] Frank, A. G., *Latin America: Underdevelopment or Revolution.* New York: Monthly Review Press, 1969.
[71] Frank, A. G., *Lumpen-Bourgeoisie and Lumpen-Development: Dependency, Class and Politics in Latin America.* New York: Monthly Review Press, 1972.
[72] Frank, A. G., *On Capitalist Underdevelopment.* Oxford: Oxford University Press, 1975.
**[73] Frank, A. G., *Reflections of the World Economic Crisis.* New York: Monthly Review Press, 1981.
**[74] Froebel, F., J Heinrich, and O. Kaye, *The New International Division of Labor.* Cambridge, Eng.: Cambridge University Press, 1980.
**[75] Furtado, C., *Economic Development of Latin America: A Survey from Colonial Times to the Cuban Revolution,* trans. by S. Macedo. Cambridge U. Press, 1970.
**[76] Gadgill, D. R., *The Industrial Evolution of India in Recent Times: 1860–1939.* Bombay: Oxford University Press, 1971.
[77] Gallagher, J., and R. Robinson, "The Imperialism of Free Trade," in *Imperialism,* ed. by W. R. Lewis. New York: New Viewpoints, 1976.
**[78] Gerschenkron, A., "Economic Backwardness in Historical Perspectives" in *Economic Backwardness in Historical Perspective: A Book of Essays.* Cambridge, Mass.: Harvard University Press, 1962.
**[79] Gerschenkron, A., "Notes on the Rate of Industrial Growth in Italy: 1881–1913," in *Economic Backwardness in Historical Perspective: A Book of Essays.* Cambridge, Mass.: Harvard University Press, 1962.
**[80] Gerschenkron, A., "Russia: Patterns and Problems in Development," in *Economic Backwardness in Historical Perspective: A Book of Essays,* Cambridge, Mass.: Harvard University Press, 1962.
**[81] Giddens, A., *A Contemporary Critique of Historical Materialism: Power, Property, and the State.* Berkeley: University of California Press, 1981.
[82] Gilpin, R., *U.S. Power and the Multinational Corporation: The Political Economy of Foreign Direct Investment.* New York: Basic Books, 1975.
*[83] Goulbourne, H. (ED.), *Politics and State in the Third World.* London: Macmillan, 1979.
[84] Gould, S. J., "Between You and Your Genes," *New York Review of Books* **31** (August 16, 1984), 30–2.
[85] Hamilton, N. L., "Mexico: The Limits of State Autonomy," *Latin American Perspectives* **2** (Summer 1975), 81–108.
[86] Hargreaves, J. D., *The End of Colonial Rule in West Africa: Essays in Contemporary History.* New York: Harper and Row, 1979.

[87] Harris, N., *Of Bread and Guns: the World Economy in Crisis*. Harmondsworth, Eng.: Penguin Books, 1983.
**[88] Hayter, T., *The Creation of World Poverty: An Alternative View to the Brandt Report*. London: Pluto Press, 1981.
*[89] Hilferding, R., *Finance Capital*, trans. by M. Watnick and S. Gordon. London: Routledge and Kegan Paul, 1981.
[90] Himmelweit, S., "Value Relations and Divisions Within the Working Class," *Science and Society* **48 (Fall 1984), 323–43.
**[91] Hinton, J., "The Rise of a Mass Labour Movement: Growth and Limits," in *A History of British Industrial Relatives*, ed. by C. Wrigley. Amherst, Mass.: University of Massachusetts Press, 1982.
**[92] Hobson, J., *Imperialism: A Study*. London: George Allen & Unwin, 1954.
**[93] Horowitz, I. L., *Beyond Empire and Revolution: Militarization and Consolidation in the Third World*. New York: Oxford University Press, 1982.
*[94] Hymer, S., "The Multinational Corporation and the Law of Uneven Development," in *Economics and World from the 1970s to the 1990s*, ed. by J. Bhagwati. Basingstoke, Eng.: Macmillan, 1972.
**[95] Itoh, M., *Value and Crisis: Essays on Marxian Economics in Japan*. London: Pluto Press, 1980.
[96] Jalee, P., *The Third World in World Ecomomy*. New York: Monthly Review Press, 1969.
[97] Jelavich, C., and B. Jelavich, *The Establishment of the Balkan National States, 1804–1920*. Seattle: University of Washington Press, 1977.
[98] Jenkins, R., "Divisions over the International Division of Labour," *Capital and Class* **22 (Spring 1984), 28–57.
**[99] Jessup, B., *The Capitalist State*. New York: New York University Press, 1982.
*[100] Keat, R., and J. Urry, *Social Theory as Science*. London: Routledge and Kegan Paul, 1975.
*[101] Kemp, T., *Theories of Imperialism*. London: Bookprint Ltd., 1967.
[102] Kidron, M., *Capitalism and Theory*. London: Pluto Press, 1974.
*[103] Kidron, M., "Imperialism: Highest Stage But One," *International Socialism* **61** (June 1973).
*[104] Kiernan, V. G., "The Marxist Theory of Imperialism and Its Historical Formation," in *Marxism and Imperialism*. New York: St. Martin's Press, 1975.
*[105] Kindleberger, C. P., *The World in Depression*. London: Allen Lane, 1973.
[106] Kirsanov, A., *The USA and Western Europe: Economic Relations after 1975*. Moscow: Progress Publishers, 1975.
[107] Kolko, J., and G. Kolko: *The Limits of Power: The World and United States Foreign Policy, 1945–54*. New York: Harper and Row, 1972.
*[108] Lawrence, R. Z., *Can America Compete?* Washington, D.C.: The Brookings Institution, 1984.
*[109] Lebon, A., and G. Falchi, "New Developments in Intra-European Migration since 1974," *International Migration Review* **14** (Winter 1980), 539–79.
*[110] Leiken, R. S. (ED.), *Central America: Anatomy of Conflict*. New York, Pergamon Press, 1984.
[111] Lenin, V. I., "Address to the Second All-Russia Congress of Communist Organizations of the Peoples of the East," in *Collected Works, Vol. 30*. Moscow: Foreign Languages Publishing House, 1965.
[112] Lenin, V. I., *The Development of Capitalism in Russia*, in *Collected Works*, vol. 3. Moscow: Foreign Languages Publishing House, 1960.

*[113] Lenin, V. I., *Imperialism: The Highest Stage of Capitalism.* Moscow: Progress Publishers, 1970.

[114] Lenin, V. I., "Preliminary Draft Theses on the National and the Colonial Questions: For the Second Congress of the Communist International," in *Collected Works, Vol. 31.* Moscow: Foreign Languages Publishing House, 1966.

[115] Lenin, V. I., "Report of the Commission on the National and the Colonial Questions, July 26, 1920," in *Collected Works,* vol. 31. Moscow; Foreign Languages Publishing House, 1966.

**[116] Lewis, G. K., *Puerto Rico: Freedom and Power in the Caribbean.* New York: Monthly Review Press, 1963.

[117] Lewis, J. P., and V. Kallab (Eds.): *U.S. Foreign Policy and the Third World Agenda 1983.* New York: Praeger, 1983.

*[118] Lipietz, A., "Imperialism or the Beast of the Apocalypse," *Capital and Class* **22** (Spring 1984), 45–66.

*[119] Loewy, M., *The Politics of Combined and Uneven Development: The Theory of Permanent Revolution.* London: Verso, 1981.

[120] Lotta, R., *America in Decline* (Chicago: Banner Press, 1984).

*[121] Luxemburg, R., *The Accumulation of Capital,* trans. by A. Schwarzchild. New York: Monthly Review Press, 1964.

*[122] Magdoff, H., *Imperialism: From the Colonial Age to the Present.* New York: Monthly Review Press, 1975.

*[123] Magdoff, H., "Is Imperialism Really Necessary?" in *Imperialism: From the Colonial Age to the Present.* New York: Monthly Review Press, 1978.

**[124] Mandel, E., *Late Capitalism.* London: Verso, 1978.

[125] Marcussen, H. S., and J. E. Torp, *Internationalization of Capital: Prospects for the Third World: A Re-examination of Dependency Theory.* London: Zed Press, 1982.

**[126] Marx, K., *Capital, vol. I.* New York, Vintage Books, 1977.

[127] Marx, K., *Capital, vol. II.* London: New Left Review, 1978.

[128] Marx, K., "Future Results of British Rule in India," in *Karl Marx and Frederick Engels, Selected Works, vol. I.* Moscow: Progress Publishers, 1969.

**[129] Marx, K., *The Grundrisse: Introduction to the Critique of Political Economy.* Middlesex, Eng.: Pelican Books, 1973.

**[130] Marx, K., and F. Engels: "The Communist Manifesto," in *The Marx-Engels Reader,* ed. by R. Tucker. New York: W. W. Norton, 1978.

[131] Melman, S., *The Permanent War Economy: American Capitalism in Decline.* New York: Simon and Schuster, 1974.

[132] Melotti, U., *Marx and the Third World.* London: Macmillan Press, 1977.

**[133] Memmi, A., *The Colonizer and the Colonized.* New York: The Orion Press, 1965.

[134] Mills, C. W., *The Power Elite.* New York: Oxford University Press, 1959.

[135] Mommsen, W. J., *Theories of Imperialism: A Critical Assessment of the Various Interpretations of Modern Imperialism,* trans. by P. S. Falla. New York: Random House, 1980.

[136] Moore, B., *Social Origins of Dictatorship and Democracy.* Boston: Beacon Press, 1966.

[137] Murphy, C., *The Emergence of NIEO Ideology.* Boulder, Colo.: Westview Press, 1984.

**[138] Nabudere, D., *The Political Economy of Imperialism.* London: Zed Press, 1977.

**[139] North, D. C., *Growth and Welfare in the American Past: A New Economic History*. Englewood Cliffs, N.J., Prentice Hall, 1966.
*[140] O'Connor, J., "The Meaning of Economic Imperialism," in *The Corporations and the State: Essays in the Theory of Capitalism and Imperialism*. New York: Harper and Row, 1974.
**[141] OECD: *World Economic Interdependence and the Evolving North-South Relationship*. Paris: OECD, 1983.
[142] Olle, W., and W. Schoeller, "Direct Investment Monopoly Theories of Imperialism," *Captial and Class* 16 (Spring 1982), 41–60.
[143] Owen, R., and B. Sutcliffe (Eds.), *Studies in the Theory of Imperialism*. London: Longman Group, 1972.
*[144] Palloix, C., "The Self-Expansion of Capital on a World Scale," *Review of Radical Political Economics* 9 (Summer 1977), 1–28.
*[145] Parboni, R., *The Dollar and Its Rivals,* trans. by Jon Rothschild. London: NLB, 1981.
[146] Parsons, H. L. (ED.), *Marx and Engels on Ecology*. Westport, Conn.: Greenwood Press, 1977.
[147] Petras, J., F. and M. H. Morley, "The Imperial State," in *Class, State and Power in the Third World*. London: Zed Press, 1981.
[148] Phillips, R., "The Role of the International Monetary Fund in the Post-Bretton Woods Era," *Review of Radical Political Economics* 15 (Summer 1983), 59–81.
**[149] Poulantzas, N., *Political Power and Social Classes*. London: NLB, 1975.
**[150] Prebisch, R., "Commercial Policy in the Underdeveloped Countries," *American Economic Review* 49 (May 1959).
*[151] Radice, H., "The National Economy: A Keynesian Myth?" *Capital and Class* 22 (Spring 1984), 111–140.
[152] Rainnie, A. F., "Combined and Uneven Development in the Clothing Industry: The Effects of Competition on Accumulation," *Capital and Class* 22 (Spring 1984), 141–156.
[153] Rhodes, R. I. (Ed.), *Imperialism and Underdevelopment*. New York: Monthly Review Press, 1970.
**[154] Robinson, J., "Introduction," in *The Accumulation of Capital,* by R. Luxemburg. New York: Monthly Review Press, 1964.
[155] Rodney, W., *How Europe Underdeveloped Africa*. Washington, D.C.: Howard University Press, 1974.
**[156] Roemer, J., *Analytic Foundations of Marxian Economic Theory*. New York: Cambridge University Press, 1981.
**[157] Roemer, J., "New Directions in the Marxian Theory of Exploitation and Class," *Politics and Society* 11 (1982), 253–88.
**[158] Roemer, J., "Unequal Exchange, Labor Migration, and International Capital Flows: A Theoretical Synthesis," in *Marxism, Central Planning, and the Soviet Economy: Economic Essays in Honor of Alexander Erlich,* ed. by P. Desai. Cambridge, Mass.: MIT Press, 1983.
**[159] Rubin, I. I., *Essays on Marx's Theory of Value*. Montreal: Black Rose Books, 1973.
**[160] Salvadori, M., *Karl Kautsky and the Socialist Revolution,* trans. by J. Rothchild. London: NLB, 1979.
[161] Sampson, A., *The Arms Bazaar, From Lebanon to Lockheed*. New York: The Viking Press, 1977.
*[162] Saul, J. S., "The State in Post-colonial Societies: Tanzania," in *Politics and State in the Third World,* ed. by H. Goulbourne. London: Macmillan, 1979.

 *[163] Schumpeter, J., "The Sociology of Imperialisms," in *Imperialism and Social Classes,* ed. by P. Sweezy. New York: Augustus M. Kelley, 1951.

  [164] Shirer, W. L., *The Rise and Fall of the Third Reich.* Greenwich, Conn., Simon and Schuster, 1960.

**[165] Sivard, R. L., *World Military and Social Expenditures.* Leesburg, Va., World Priorities, various annual editions.

  [166] Smith, D., and R. Smith, *The Economics of Militarism.* London: Pluto Press, 1983.

  [167] Smith, D. M., *Italy, A Modern History.* Ann Arbor, University of Michigan Press, 1959.

**[168] Smith, T., *The Pattern of Imperialism: The United States, Great Britain and the Late Industrializing World since 1815.* Cambridge, Eng.: Cambridge University Press, 1981.

**[169] Stalin, J., "Problems of Leninism," in *Selected Works.* Davis, Calif.: Cardinal Publishers, 1971.

**[170] Sternberg, F., *Der Imperialismus.* Berlin: Malik-Verlag, 1926.

 *[171] Szymanski, A., *The Logic of Imperialism.* New York: Praeger, 1981.

  [172] Tanzer, M., *The Political Economy of International Oil and the Underdeveloped Countries.* Boston: Beacon Press, 1969.

**[173] Tanzer, M., *The Race for Resources: Continuing Struggles over Minerals and Fuels.* New York: Monthly Review Press, 1980.

**[174] Tanzer, M., and S. Zorn, "Opec's Decade: Has It Made a Difference?", *Monthly Review* 3 (May 1984), 31–43.

**[175] Taylor, J. G., *From Modernization to Modes of Production: A Critique of the Sociologies of Development and Underdevelopment.* London: Macmillan Press, 1979.

 *[176] Thompson, E. P., "Europe: The Weak Link in the Cold War," in *Exterminism and Cold War,* London: Verso, 1982.

 *[177] Thompson, E. P., "Notes on Exterminism, The Last Stage of Civilization," in *Exterminism and Cold War.* London: Verso, 1982.

**[178] Thompson, E. P., and D. Smith (Eds.), *Protest and Survive.* New York: Monthly Review Press, 1981.

  [179] Thornton, A. P., *Imperialism in the Twentieth Century.* Minneapolis, Minn.: University of Minnesota Press, 1977.

  [180] Thurow, L., "Losing the Economic Race," *New York Review of Books* **31** (September 27, 1984), 29–31.

**[181] UNCTAD, "An Integrated Programme for Commodities and Indexation of Prices," in *The New International Economic Order: Confrontation or Cooperation between North and South.* Boulder, Colo.: Westview Press, 1977.

**[182] UNESCO: *Statistical Yearbook 1983, vol. III.* Paris: UNESCO, 1983.

**[183] United Nations: *Multinational Corporations in World Development.* New York: United Nations, 1973.

**[184] Veblen, T., *Imperial Germany and the Industrial Revolution.* New York: Macmillan, 1915.

**[185] Vernon, R., *Sovereignty at Bay: The Multinational Spread of U.S. Enterprises.* New York: Basic Books, 1971.

 *[186] Wallerstein, I., "Crisis in Transition," in *Dynamics of Global Crisis.* New York: Monthly Review Press, 1982.

 *[187] Wallerstein, I., "The Rise and Future Demise of the World Capitalist Systems: Concepts for Comparative Analysis," in *The Capitalist World*

Economy: *Essays by Immanuel Wallerstein.* Cambridge, Eng.: Cambridge University Press, 1979.
[188] Warren, B., *Imperialism*: *Pioneer of Capitalism.* London: NLB, 1980.
[189] Weber, M., "Structures of Power," in *From Max Weber,* ed. by H. H. Gerth and C. W. Mills. New York: Oxford University Press, 1958.
[190] White, C., "Recent Debates in Vietnamese Development Policy," in *Revolutionary Socialist Development in the Third World,* ed. by G. White, R. Murray and C. White. Brighton, Eng.: Wheatsheaf Books, 1983.
[191] Williams, W. A., *Empire as a Way of Life.* New York: Oxford University Press, 1980.
[192] Willoughby, J., "The Changing Role of Protection in the World Economy," *Cambridge Journal of Economics* 6 (June 1982), 195–211.
[193] Willoughby, J., "The Lenin-Kautsky Unity-Rivalry Debate," *Review of Radical Political Economics* 11 (Winter 1979), 91–101.
[194] Willoughby, J., "Must Monetarism Persist? The Internationalization of Capital and the Future of Macroeconomic Policy," *Science and Society,* 49 (Fall 1985), 287–314.
[195] World Bank: *World Development Report* 1983. Washington, D.C.: IBRD, 1983.
[196] World Bank: *World Development Report* 1984. Washington, D.C.: IBRD, 1984.

Indicates books and papers considered by the author essential to the understanding of the topics covered in this book.
Indicates all publications mentioned in the text but not covered by a single asterisk.
References not preceded by an asterisk are books and papers considered by the author to be interesting and relevant.

INDEX

For Product Safety Concerns and Information please contact our EU
representative GPSR@taylorandfrancis.com Taylor & Francis Verlag GmbH,
Kaufingerstraße 24, 80331 München, Germany

Printed and bound by CPI Group (UK) Ltd, Croydon, CR0 4YY
11/04/2025
01844009-0012